The God
of the
Breakthrough
Will Visit
Your House

JERRY SAVELLE

The God of the Breakthrough
Will Visit Your House

ISBN 0-9702911-3-2
Unless otherwise stated, all Scripture quotations
are taken from The King James Version
of the Bible.

Jerry Savelle Ministries International
P.O. Box 748
Crowley, TX 76036
(817) 297-3155
www.jsmi.org

Second Printing – 2005

Table of Contents

Introduction

This book is unlike any other book I've written before. I am going to share with you, not a message, but a mandate I received from the Lord that has changed the course of my destiny. And I believe it will change yours, too. I have been in ministry since 1969, and I have experienced three very distinct supernatural visitations of the Lord during that time. In each of those visitations, the Lord gave me very clear instructions to teach the body of Christ. As I share in detail in this book the instructions the Lord gave me, I believe that you will open your heart to receive and allow the Holy Spirit to get you in position for the God of the breakthrough to visit your house!

What is so unique about each of the visitations I received is, first of all, I did not ask for them. I know preachers who are constantly asking for a vision of Jesus. I never asked for it. Secondly, it caught me totally off guard. I had no idea it was going to happen. God didn't give me some kind of signal. I didn't expect it. I didn't know it was going to happen. And thirdly, I really wasn't doing anything "super-spiritual" when it happened.

Over the years, I have been a little hesitant to talk about some of the visions and revelations I have experienced in ministry. Sometimes, the reason is because of the foolishness you hear from some people who think they've had a revelation from the Lord and all it was – was them. I've always been on the overly protective side.

The Apostle Paul told us that during his walk with God,

there were times when he experienced special manifestations of the Lord through visions and revelations.

It is not expedient for me doubtless to glory. I will come to visions and revelations of the Lord.

2 Corinthians 12:1

In no way am I trying to compare myself with the Apostle Paul. But, I am going to be bold to tell you that I too have experienced some visions and revelations of the Lord. When I read that verse, I can identify with what he was saying.

He explains in Galatians 1:11-12, **But I certify you, brethren, that the gospel which was preached of me is not after man. For I neither received it of man, neither was I taught it, but by the revelation of Jesus Christ.**

In other words Paul is saying, "What I have been preaching to you, I did not get from another man. It did not come by natural human means. I didn't read somebody's book or listen to somebody's tape. Those things that I've been saying to you, I got by revelation of Jesus Christ Himself" (Author's paraphrase).

The Amplified says it this way, **For I want you to know, brethren, that the gospel which was proclaimed and made known by me is not man's Gospel [a human invention, according to or patterned after any human standard]. For indeed I did not receive it from man, nor was I taught it but [it came to me] ...**

In each of my visitations, once I received the Word from God, He said, "I will hold you responsible for teaching this to the body of Christ."

So now I have an assignment. I have a mandate. I will be very frank and very honest with you, there have been times when I was preaching these revelations, and I would feel uncomfortable doing so because of what people might think. I said, "Lord, I'm going to put this on the shelf right now."

He never said, "Fine, son. That will be just fine."

In fact, He never said anything, which should have given me a clue. It wasn't alright with the Lord, so I must share with you what the Lord gave to me in each of those life-changing visitations.

The First Visitation

The first visitation was in October 1981, in Charlotte, North Carolina. I was ministering at Kenneth Copeland's East Coast Believers' Convention. It was a Thursday afternoon. I had just finished my session and my wife, Carolyn, and I went back to the hotel. Carolyn said, "Jerry, I'm going to rest for a little while. Are you going to take a nap?"

I said, "No. I'm just going to put on my robe and sit in the living room and relax until it is time to get dressed and go to the service."

I sat down on the sofa and propped my feet up on the coffee table. I put my hands behind my head and leaned back and was almost in a state of dozing off. I wasn't praying in the spirit. I didn't have my Bible next to my chest. I was tired. I was just sitting there minding my own business. All of a sudden, the Shekinah Glory of God completely consumed that room. It filled the atmosphere.

In that cloud of glory, Jesus spoke, and here is what He said: "My people are experiencing financial famine and I am going to reveal to you the keys that will bring them out."

It seemed like He talked to me for hours, but it turned out to be only minutes.

I sat there basking in this glory, literally shaking under the power of God and it eventually awakened Carolyn. She came in the room and her opening remark was, "What is going on in here?"

I said, "Carolyn, Jesus just visited me."

She sensed the anointing that was still in the room and we both just lifted our hands and began to pray in the Holy Ghost. In a little while, it was time to get dress and go over to the service. I didn't call Brother Copeland and tell him what had happened. I got dressed, went over to the meeting, and sat on the front row with the other speakers. Brother Copeland went up to the platform and he sang a couple of songs. He laid his Bible down and said, "Now, let's open our Bibles ..." and then he didn't say anything else.

"Let's open our Bibles ..." he said again. Finally, he looked at me and said, "... Jerry ... God visited you today. Come tell us what He said."

He closed his Bible and said, "Somebody bring me a chair." And he placed it right there next to the podium. I walked up and preached exactly what the Lord told me that evening on the keys to overcoming financial famine. God told me to title it, "Sowing in Famine."

It was one of the strongest anointings I had ever operated in up to that time. Financial miracles took place in that service that very night! The financial breakthroughs and testimonies that we received everywhere I preached it were some of the most amazing breakthroughs I'd ever heard about in my life. Obviously, it was God.

Going into 1982, I preached it everywhere I went. In fact, the Spirit of God gave me this phrase, "Something new in '82. Financially free by '83." I preached it all over the world.

Everywhere I went, it was the same. Financial breakthroughs everywhere. It was awesome.

Later, around 1987, some scandals came to some major ministries. I did not want anybody thinking that Jerry Savelle was just preaching sermons to "make money." So, I put that message on the shelf. God never told me to do it, I just said, "If it is O.K. with you Lord, I'm going to put it on the shelf until all the mess blows over and then I'll preach it again." He never said that was fine. He never said a word. Consequently, my disobedience caused our ministry to take a nosedive financially!

The Second Visitation

The second visitation came November 1992, in Bournemouth, England, at the Kenneth Copeland Believers' Convention. I went back to my hotel room after the service, preparing to go to bed and Jesus visited me again. I didn't expect it. I didn't ask for it.

This time He said, "My people are living in survival mode and it's not My best for their lives. I'm going to reveal to you the keys that will move them into supernatural increase and restoration." He then spoke to me about those keys and He told me, "I'm holding you responsible for teaching this everywhere you go."

The same thing happened the next night . . . Brother Copeland was preaching and stopped right in the middle of the sermon and said, "Jerry, did God visit you again?"

I said, "Yes, He did."

He said, "Well, get up here and tell us what He said."

He closed his Bible and allowed me to preach the message that Jesus had given me.

I preached on supernatural increase and restoration everywhere I went and our ministry recovered everything Satan had stolen from us. It was supernatural.

The Third Visitation

The third visitation came on a Wednesday night, February 2004, in Liberty, Texas. When I arrived there, I was very tired. I went to my hotel room and laid down. I knew if I didn't get a nap before the service that night, I was not going to be able to give the people my best.

I laid down in that little room in Liberty, Texas, and was awakened with my third visitation of the Lord. I didn't expect it. I didn't know it was going to happen.

This time the Lord said to me, "My people have been overwhelmed by financial attacks. Tell them that if they will apply the keys that I will reveal to you, then the God of the Breakthrough will visit their house."

It's interesting to me that all three visitations that I've experienced have had to do with finances. The strongest anointing that I walk in is when I'm teaching on finances in the body of Christ. Even though there are a lot of other things I enjoy preaching and teaching, the strongest anointing I've ever operated in is when I am teaching the body of Christ how to win financially.

I've also noticed that when I'm teaching these principles, then I'm always winning financially as well. Presently, we are experiencing some of the greatest breakthroughs that we've ever experienced.

I have an assignment on my life and I'm not going to

disobey God ever again. The Lord said, "I am holding you responsible for teaching these keys."

I'm preaching it everywhere I go. No matter what anybody else thinks, I am not getting off of my mandate ever again.

My assignment in this book is to share these keys with you and show you how to get into position for the God of the Breakthrough to visit your house!

PART

1

The First Visitation

1 "Does anyone know I exist?"

When you're going through a challenging time (and we all do), it can be one of the loneliest feelings in the world. Whether it's a threat in your marriage, a struggle in your finances, or the pressure of day-to-day living, when you're the one going through it, you begin to wonder, "Does anyone know I exist? And if they do, does anybody care?"

Have you ever felt like God has forgotten your address? Satan has a way of making you feel absolutely hopeless. He'll tell you that nobody cares, nobody is praying for you, and your circumstances will never change. He is a liar. He is incapable of telling the truth.

God hasn't forgotten you. In fact, He is mindful of you. Not only that, but the Bible tells us that Jesus of Nazareth ever lives to make intercession for us (Hebrews 7:25). That means His mind is on you. If Jesus is praying for you, then you can count on it, His prayers are heard in heaven. If anyone gets their prayers answered, it has to be Jesus. Read what the Psalmist

David had to say about how much God cares about us.

O Israel, trust thou in the Lord: he is their help and their shield. O house of Aaron, trust in the Lord: he is their help and their shield. Ye that fear the LORD, trust in the LORD: he is their help and their shield. The LORD hath been mindful of us: he will bless us; he will bless the house of Israel; he will bless the house of Aaron. He will bless them that fear the LORD, both small and great. The LORD shall increase you more and more, you and your children.

Psalm 115:9-14

Have you ever gone to someone in hard times and said, "I need help?" And they said, "I'd love to help you but I can't . . ." Let me tell you right now that you will never hear God say that to you. Not one time will you approach the throne of God and say, "God, I need help financially" only to have Him say, "I'd love to help you but you don't understand . . . we've got a depression going on up here. I had to lay Jesus off this morning. The angels are on strike. I'm going to have to sell the Pearly Gates to pay the note on the throne room. I'd love to help you but you don't understand, we're a little short up here today!!"

No!! He said that He would supply all your need according to His riches in glory by Christ Jesus (Philippians 4:19)! God could walk in your house right now and supernaturally bless you beyond your wildest dreams financially and it would not put a dent in His capital reserves. He is El Shaddai not "El Cheapo." And He wants to bless you!

"...The Lord hath been mindful of us ..." I don't know about you but it has always been a great comfort to me to know somebody has been mindful of me. Doesn't it help you when you're being challenged and someone comes up to you, pats you on the back, and says, "You're going to make it. I'm praying for you"?

It's nice to know that someone has you on their mind. It's nice to know the people in your church have you on their minds. The Bible says that the **Lord** has you on His mind. There's not one moment in your day that God doesn't have you on His mind.

There are scriptures that reveal what God thinks about you. One particular verse says that His thoughts about you are good and favorable and positive. "His thoughts are for an expected end. A wonderful future" (Jeremiah 29:11).

Many people have a wrong image of God. They think that God is sitting up there figuring out ways to hurt people. I was told that growing up. I remember being told in religious circles that God would break your neck to teach you something, or God would put cancer on you so it would glorify Him. God's not sitting on His throne thinking of ways that He can hurt you. God's not sitting on His throne trying to figure out what sickness it will take to destroy you. He's not ... but Satan is! God's thoughts are good. He's a good God. He is the Deliverer. He's not the destroyer. He's the Restorer; not the thief.

"Have you heard what the devil did?"

I remember the early years of my Christianity, I would be sitting in a church service and people would go forward to share their testimonies. They would stand up and "testify." Most of the time, they magnified the devil rather than giving any glory to God. They would spend an hour and a half on what the devil was doing and right at the end, they would say, "But we all know that our God's able."

It didn't mean a whole lot after an hour and a half of what the devil had been doing. "The Devil visited our house last week. Stole my husband's job, stole all our money, wrecked the car, the kids are sick. We're going broke, losing everything. It's been a hard week. Y'all pray that we'll hold out unto the end. Bless His Holy Name! We know He is able."

Those kinds of testimonies never inspired me. That's the reason I stayed out of church most of the time. I thought, "Dear God, I've got enough trouble as it is. Why would I want to hang around this bunch?" Their favorite closing remark was always, "Our God is able."

I would hear people say, "Our God is able," and I would walk up to them and say, "But will He?"

They would reply, "Oh, you never know what God will do."

I'd say, "Well, His Word says, 'He will bless us.'"

"Oh, if it be His will, He will."

"Well, He just said what His will is . . . He said, 'I will bless you,'" I'd say. And most of the time they would look at me as though I was out of my mind. I can say with all confidence that I'm going to be blessed. I expect to be blessed.

"How do you know, Jerry? You can't foresee the future. You don't know what lies ahead."

I don't know everything about what lies ahead but I do know how it's going to turn out. "Jerry will be blessed." Why? Because God said so!

I choose to believe His Word and I expect His blessings to come into my life.

Psalm 115:12 says, **The Lord hath been mindful of us: he will bless us: he will bless the house of Israel; he will bless the house of Aaron.** In other words, God will bless His covenant people.

This doesn't just work for a few selected people. God is no respecter of persons. There is no limit to how much God wants to increase your life. God rewards those who walk uprightly before Him and those who diligently seek Him.

God doesn't love me any more than He loves you. He doesn't love someone else any more than He loves you. God is not going down the line saying, "I love you, I love you not . . . I love you, I love you not . . ."

When you woke up this morning, God had you on His mind! God has you on His mind right now. He already has your future planned!! He has a wonderful destiny for you, praise God!! And it's not one of lack or failure or disease! It is of victory, hallelujah!

Since 1969, when I surrendered my life to the Lord, my life has been a story of increase!! I'm increasing in my ability to hear God! I'm increasing in revelation knowledge! I'm increasing in my sensitivity to the Holy Spirit! I'm increasing financially! My children are blessed. I am enjoying my rights as a child of God ... and you should, too. If you stood next to that man I was in 1968 and the man that I am today, you would see that they don't resemble. They don't look anything alike. They don't think alike. They don't act alike. They don't believe alike. One was failing and on his way to hell and the other is a winner and on his way to heaven!

What happened? Increase. The Lord brought increase into my life and He'll do it for you, too.

Are you satisfied with where you are?

Though thy beginning was small, yet thy latter end should greatly increase.

Job 8:7

I was a nobody, insignificant, just a little speck on this planet! But God found this nobody out on North Market Avenue in a paint and body shop in Shreveport, Louisiana, and said, "You know, I believe I can use that nobody!"

I said, "Do You have any idea what You are getting when You get me?"

He said, "Don't worry about it, I am a Master at making champions out of nobodies!"

If you've ever been called a nobody, then you qualify to become a champion.

For I know the thoughts that I think toward you, saith the Lord, thoughts of peace, and not of evil, to give you an expected end.

Jeremiah 29:11

The Amplified says: **...to give you hope in your final outcome.**

God doesn't have one evil thought in His mind regarding you. As I mentioned before, God is not the one who is planning disaster or destruction for your life. Failure is not in the plan of God for any of His children. God's desire and God's plan is that you become successful in every endeavor in life. God wants you to live in health; and He wants you to succeed and to be prosperous.

You and I have an adversary who is persistent. He comes to steal, kill, and destroy (John 10:10). But that doesn't mean that you have to lie down, roll over, play dead, and let him do it. He seeks whom he may devour, so just say to him, "You may not devour me!"

We've had our share of adversity and we will continue to face adversity, but adversity has a way of bringing out the champion that is on the inside of you. When you were born again, you were born to be a champion; you were born to be a winner. You are not a loser. Don't allow anyone to convince you that you are a loser.

No matter how miserable your life may be at this very moment, God has a plan to turn your life around. When you're distressed, if you won't run from God but run to Him, then He can and He will turn your captivity around.

And it shall come to pass, that before they call, I will answer; and while they are yet speaking, I will hear.

Isaiah 65:24

God's declaring that before you can utter the very first word of your prayer, He's already preparing a solution or a way out of your circumstances. While you are still calling on Him, He's already involved in dispatching His angels to go forth and change your circumstances. Why? Because it's never God's will that you fail. It's never God's will that you stay in captivity. It's never God's will that you stay in bondage.

In fact, while you're reading this book, angels are out there working in your behalf. Hallelujah! The miracle you need, the manifestation you're believing for could happen before you finish reading this book. Today could be your due season. Today could be your appointed time. "Well, what if it's not today, Jerry?" Well, thank God there's always tomorrow.

I'm prepared to stand for my miracle. In fact, I am an expert at standing. My name is Jerry, "having done all to stand – stand," Savelle. I know how to stand and God has always been faithful!

Now thanks be unto God, which always causeth us to triumph in Christ, . . .

2 Corinthians 2:14

Notice the word **always**. That's the will of God. It's never the will of God that you and I win a few — lose a few. God's will is that we triumph **always**. No matter how impossible your circumstances look at this very moment, don't ever give up until you triumph! I don't care if you fall and stumble seven times, get up eight and go again! Don't accept defeat. Don't accept anything but triumph.

Setbacks are not permanent. They are temporary. Setbacks can become stepping-stones to greater victories.

Are you qualified?

I don't care what your background is, and I don't care if you've never won at anything in life, it's not too late! You are a winner! You have the blood of Jesus running through your veins. You are a champion on the inside, and it's time that the devil begins to see that champion rise up on the outside. It's time to get out of survival mentality and begin to believe God for breakthrough in every area of your life.

Your background has nothing to do with whether or not you qualify to be a champion in life. Just as long as you put your confidence and trust in God's ability to get you over, and not your own.

For ye see your calling, brethren, how that not many wise men after the flesh, not many mighty, not many noble, are called: But God hath chosen the foolish things of the world to confound the wise; and God hath chosen the weak things of the world to confound the things which are mighty; And base things of the world, and things which are despised, hath God chosen, yea, and things which are not, to bring to nought things that are: That no flesh should glory in his presence.

I Corinthians 1:26-29

God is not looking for those who have all the credentials or who have all the education that the world says one must have to qualify. There's nothing wrong with education, but God's not saying that you have to be an expert in a particular field before He can use you and bless you. God's saying, "Whatever the world says can't be used, I can use." Do you qualify? If the world says there is absolutely no hope for you, then God sees a candidate. When your parents, your relatives, and your friends think that you will never amount to anything, God says, "there's a potential champion!"

You are not a loser; you are a winner. You are not a failure; you are a champion! The New Burkley version says, **God also has chosen the world's insignificant and despised people and nobodies, in order to bring to nothing those who amount to something. So that nobody may boast in the presence of God.**

On the inside of you is unlimited potential! God is looking for people in these last days who will tap that potential and get maximum results with it.

It's time for you to get over all the negative words that have been spoken over you! Get over all your previous mistakes! Get over all your past failures! God says that He can use you. He needs you. He wants you. You're a champion!

God never looks on the outward appearance, He sees what's on the inside.

. . . Look not on his countenance . . . for the Lord seeth not as man seeth; for man looketh on the outward appearance, but the Lord looketh on the heart.
I Samuel 16:7

So what if your family doesn't think these things can happen to you. So what if your friends laugh and persecute you. So what if they can't see what God sees. So what if there's never been any indication in your life that you are a potential champion. So what if you've failed at everything you've ever attempted in days past. If God says you are a champion, you're a champion. If God says you can, then you can!

Others may never see what God sees in you. You have to learn to not be moved by what you see, by what you hear, nor by what you feel. Some of my relatives thought I'd lost my mind when I first came to the Lord. But now, when they are in need, they call the one "who lost his mind." Why? Because the little nobody has become a champion, hallelujah!

Even though God may call you a champion, you may not become that champion in the next 24 hours. But if you'll be faithful to what the Word of God says and not allow others to distract you or discourage you, then the champion that's on the inside is going to come to the surface.

Today you may be in debt up to your eyeballs. You may be the most miserable person in the world. You may not be able to remember the last time you succeeded at anything, but down on the inside of you there is a champion that is ready to come out. So don't give up, don't be discouraged, and don't quit.

The very adversity you're experiencing today could become the stepping stone to your greatest victory! In other words, you can turn every test into a testimony. God is a master at making champions out of nobodies. Let Him make one out of you. Does anybody know you exist? Yes, the Creator of this Universe, the Very One who gave you life cares about every detail of your life. He doesn't want you barely surviving in any area of your life . . . but thriving in all areas. Before you ever experience a breakthrough in your life, you must first see yourself the way God sees you, and expect Him to visit your house.

2 How to get God to answer your prayers

My daughters are in their thirties, but to this very day, I still like it when they come into my house, sit on my knee, and tell me how much they love me. They think I'm the best Dad, the strongest Dad, and the cutest Dad. I promise you, before they leave, they won't have to ask for anything, I'm going to say, "Let's go shopping!"

God wants to be your Provider, but He also wants you to seek His face.

Most people seek the hand of God which is symbolic of provision. The Bible says, "Seek My face," which indicates intimacy (2 Chronicles 7:14). When you seek the Provider then His provisions always come.

It's not very comfortable, as a parent, when the only time your children want to talk to you or fellowship with you is when they are in need. "Daddy, can I talk to you? I need . . ." As a parent, wouldn't you like every once in a while for your child to say, "Daddy, I love you. I just want to spend some time with you. Can I hang around you today?"

When you and I first came to God, the first thing that came out of our mouths was not, "Oh God, I need . . ." It was, "Oh God, I love you! Jesus, I love you, thank you for changing my life. Lord, is there anything I can do for you?" There are a lot of Christians who haven't been that way in a long time and are never going to tap into the fullness of the blessings of God until they become intimate with God once again.

Jesus said that the most important thing you are to do in your life is to love God. There are three levels of love: intimacy, passion, and commitment. Intimacy comes when two people reveal themselves to each other – it gives strength to the relationship. It cannot be developed by one or two conversations. It must be on-going fellowship.

When you are passionate about someone, you refuse to allow anything to rob you of your time with that person. Why? Because the desire of your heart is to be with them. It is not a "duty" to spend time together; it is a desire! You enjoy each other's company. Intimacy and passion lead to commitment. When you are committed to someone, you are devoted to spending quality time with that person. Nothing comes between your relationship.

Yield now and be at peace with Him; Thereby good will come to you. Please receive instruction from His mouth, And establish His words in your

heart. If you return to the Almighty, you will be restored ...

Job 22:21-23a
New American Standard

We are in the days of restoration, but there are a lot of God's people who are not going to be affected by it. However, reacquainting or yielding yourself to God will put you into a position to receive increase and restoration.

Getting too busy is easy for all of us to do. I've done it! We have to discipline ourselves and rearrange our priorities. Instead of trying to fit God into our schedule, we need to work our schedule around our time with God. He must be priority in our lives!

I think some people might have to approach God the way they do when they haven't seen a friend in a long time. They may want to say, "Do you remember me?"

... they that seek the Lord shall not want any good thing.

Psalm 34:10

When you seek God, seek fellowship and intimacy with Him, good things will come into your life! You don't have to seek the "good things" – they come as a result of your relationship with God.

When your motivation for studying the Bible is so that you can "know" Him and not just to find some "secret formula," then you will discover that your relationship with Him will put you in a position to have your every need met. That's why Jesus said, **. . . seek ye first the kingdom of God . . .** or in other words, PUT GOD FIRST in your life, then **. . . all these things shall be added unto you** (Matthew 6:33).

If you would direct your heart right, And spread out your hand to Him; And your life would be brighter than noonday; Darkness would be like morning. Then you would trust, because there is hope; And you would look around, and rest securely. You would lie down and none would disturb you, and many would entreat your favor.

Job 11:13,17-19
New American Standard

Reacquainting yourself with God will bring brighter days, hope for the future, security, and favor. Don't look everywhere else for these things – look to God!

Do you remember the last time you had quality time with God? Think about the last time that you knew without a doubt God showed you something or spoke to you. If it's been so long that you have to stay up all night trying to remember, then it's time to get reacquainted!

Acquaint now thyself with him, and be at peace: thereby good shall come unto thee.

Job 22:21

Just reading the Bible religiously before you go to bed every night is not quality time! Quality time is not when one person is doing all the talking and everything they talk about is a request. If I say to a friend, "I'd like to spend some quality time with you, and here's what I want to talk to you about: I have need of this, and I'd like for you to take care of that, and if you get around to it, could you supply this? It's been good talking with you. I appreciate the quality time."

That's not quality time. The other person would like to get a word in! Just about the time he thinks you're going to be quiet for a moment and let him speak, you say, "Bye, got to go!"

Learn to listen when spending time with God. Don't do all the talking. When you hear a **"rhema"** from God, which is the Greek word meaning *an explicit word from God spoken directly to you* – it makes all the difference in your life. The rhema is what gets you over. One word from God spoken directly into your heart is worth more than 50 sermons you'll ever hear anybody preach!

How do you hear the rhema? By spending time with God. You've got to ask yourself, "Just how desperate and just how important is it for me to hear from God?" Is it important enough to do whatever it takes? Is it important enough to rearrange your schedule so that your time with Him is not stolen?

You can have all the books, tapes, and videos from every minister in America, but the most important thing is that YOU have an intimate relationship with God. You must communicate with God. Get to know your Father.

Seek the Provider, not the provision! Seek the Healer, not the healing. Seek God's face, not His hands. Get into position to receive the blessings you're entitled to, by spending time with your Father . . . that's how you get God to answer your prayers.

3 Why you're just "surviving"

I can tell you exactly why many of God's people are just surviving . . . they are not "fed up" with their situation yet. Before anything will change in your life, you've got to get "fed up" with your present condition. God is wanting to raise up an army of believers in these last days who will literally march into Satan's camp and take back everything he has stolen from them! But you've got to get fed up with the devil stealing from you! You've got to get fed up with the devil stealing everything you've got. You've got to get fed up with never having enough! Get fed up with always coming up short! It's time for supernatural increase and restoration in your life, but it won't happen until you get fed up with not having God's best in your life.

In this chapter, I want to share with you how Satan operates and how you can defeat his operations in your life.

Satan's mightiest weapon

The only way Satan can keep you from being blessed is

through deception. Deception is Satan's mightiest weapon. Outside of deception, he is helpless. If he can't deceive you, then he can't defeat you. If he can't deceive you, then he can't steal from you. According to the Word of God, one of the major ways he deceives the body of Christ is through a lack of knowledge.

My people are destroyed for a lack of knowledge...
Hosea 4:6

If you don't know that you have a right to live in health, then you will live in sickness. If you don't know you have a right to prosper, then you will live in poverty and defeat. If you don't know you have a right to be delivered, then you will live in bondage. But the moment you find out the truth, the truth will set you free!! You will begin to walk in the blessing that you are entitled to.

Obviously, Satan doesn't want you to find out what rightfully belongs to you as a child of God, and he will do everything in his power to keep you in darkness. How? Through deception.

God has done everything necessary for you and I to live an overcoming life. Jesus does not have to go to the cross again for that to take place in your life. He's already gone. He's already made provision. He's already given His Word. He's already shed His blood. The covenant is in effect and all you have to do is get into position to receive; stand your ground, and don't let the devil steal what rightfully belongs to you.

Have you ever had something stolen from you? I have. Most of us have. I can't stand a thief. Why? Because he has no regard for what I went through to get what he just stole from me.

Once, there was someone who made me a beautiful saddle for my horse, Jubilee. But one day, somebody broke into my tack room and stole my saddle. It's a good thing I wasn't around. I don't know what I would have done to that guy if I could have caught him. Whatever it might have been, I would have repented later!

That bothered me for weeks. He came onto my property, which I bought and paid for by working hard. He broke into my tack room and stole my saddles! I was really mad about this.

One day the Lord said to me, "I've never seen you so mad."

I said, "I'm real mad. If I could catch him . . ."

He said, "Why don't you act that way about the devil?"

I said, "We're not talking about the devil right now. I want that guy."

He said, "The devil steals from you and you just let him get away with it. I'm surprised with the way you're reacting to this."

He said, "You're so mad that you're hoping he'll come back, so you can catch him." He said, "I haven't seen you this way where the devil is concerned and he's stealing from you every day."

That got my attention! The devil is stealing from you and me, and most of the time, we don't even put up a fight. We might as well say, "Can I help you carry it out?" The devil's stealing from us and we just sit there and let him get away with it.

God says, "When you catch a thief, make him pay it back sevenfold!" (Proverbs 6:31).

It's time to get mad at the devil and make him pay us back seven fold.

Too expensive to mess with

Jesse Duplantis says, "It will finally get to the point that you will become too expensive for the devil to mess with." Satan's probably got warehouses full of what belongs to you and me. He's got buildings that belong to us. He's got vehicles that belong to us. He's got equipment that belongs to us. He's got finances that belong to us.

Remember the story of the two brothers, Jacob and Esau? Jacob stole his brother's birthright and his blessing, and notice what Isaac says to his son, Esau, concerning his future:

And by thy sword shalt thou live, and shalt serve thy brother; and it shall come to pass when thou shalt have the dominion, that thou shalt break his yoke from off thy neck.

Genesis 27:40

If you are ever going to get back what Satan's stolen from you, then you're going to have to live by the sword!! That sword is not a defensive weapon, it is an offensive weapon!! If you are passive, you'll never get your blessing back! You've got to be militant. You've got to be assertive. You've got to be aggressive, or you'll never get your blessing back.

. . . and it shall come to pass . . . Don't you love that? If you will live by your sword (the Word), you can count on it, this will come to pass: **. . . when thou shalt have the dominion, that thou shalt break his yoke from off thy neck.**

What is God saying here? He says that if you'll determine that you are going to live by the Word of God, then you will eventually break that yoke of bondage from off your neck.

And by your sword you shall live, and your brother you shall serve . . . (New American Standard).

God is saying, "I'm going to reverse some things. Instead of you being under subordination to the deceiver, I'll reverse it and the deceiver will now be under your lordship. Instead of the devil controlling your life, you will be controlling his. Instead of him making you miserable every day, you'll torment him every day" (Author's paraphrase).

. . . And your brother you shall serve; but it shall come about when you become restless . . .

The Texas translation for "you shall become restless," is "fed up!" Do you ever get fed up over something every once in a while? What happens when you reach the point of being "fed up?" There is an anointing that comes on you! There is a dominion that you begin to walk in and everybody within shouting distance knows you are fed up!

What happens when you're fed up? You move into action. Then what happens? You'll start getting results. Have you ever noticed what happens when a mother tells her children to clean up their room repeatedly, and they don't respond?

She tells those precious little angels, "I want you to clean up that room."

She comes back later and nothing has changed.

"I said, 'clean up the room!'" she says.

Eventually, she returns to find that still nothing has changed! What happens? Mama gets fed up! And when Mama gets fed up, there is an anointing that comes on her. Her countenance changes! Her voice changes. Her dominion takes over. She is changed into another woman! All of a sudden, she is no longer the weaker vessel! It is Samson in disguise! The kids know when Mama is fed up! I don't care if her husband weighs 372 pounds and whips everybody in the neighborhood, when Mama is fed up, he becomes a lamb.

What is <u>your</u> tolerance level?

You may not be fed up yet with Satan stealing from you!

You could be politely saying, "Oh God, make the devil get off me!" He won't. The devil won't get off of you until you get fed up with him being on you!

You're not going to change your lifestyle until you are fed up with the way you are living. You have to be fed up with your kids being on drugs. You have to get fed up with your family going to hell. You have to get fed up with never having enough and just barely scraping by. But the moment you get fed up, something happens!

When you get fed up, you're going to take that yoke off your neck! When you get fed up, there isn't any demon from hell that can hold you back!

As long as you are still tolerating it, then you're not fed up! Don't just accept your condition. Don't make provision for failure. Instead of just living with the problem, get fed up with it!

When I say fed up, I'm not talking about just psyching yourself out. No! I'm not talking about just sitting in your bedroom and saying, "I'm fed up. I'm fed up . . ." The only way you are going to reach a point of being spiritually fed up is by the entrance of God's Word! With the entrance of His Word, you begin to realize what's being stolen from you. God's Word brings light into the dark areas of your life.

When you find out what is yours by revelation of the Word of God, then you will never be passive again. Why? Because you are fed up! You'll be declaring, "No more, Satan! This is where you get out! You aren't welcome here any more! You can take your sickness and your disease and go in the Name of Jesus! Take your hands off my family, take your hands off my body, take your hands off my finances, take your hands off everything that is mine! You are history devil, and you're not welcome here any more!"

And then get back what's been stolen! Remember: Nothing changes until you get fed up with your present condition.

Pursue, overtake, and recover all!

In 1 Samuel 30, we read of David and his men who returned one day to find that their homes had been burned to the ground and the enemy had taken their wives and children.

Now my saddle is one thing, but my family, that's something else. You don't touch my wife. And you don't touch my children. I'm touchy about my family.

Can you imagine how this man must have felt? The dearest thing to him had been stolen. His privacy had been invaded. Read what the Word says about David.

Then David and the people that were with him lifted up their voice and wept, until they had no more power to weep. And David's two wives were taken captives, Ahinoam the Jezreelitess, and Abigail the wife of Nabal the Carmelite.

And David was greatly distressed; for the people

spake of stoning him, because the soul of all the people was grieved, every man for his sons and for his daughters: but David encouraged himself in the Lord his God.

I Samuel 30:4-6

After they finished crying, they all started blaming David. They wanted to stone him. I would imagine that David was sitting there thinking, "Well, I deserve to be stoned. Put me out of my misery. I didn't ask for this. I was happy when I was herding sheep. If God would have left me alone out there in that pasture, this wouldn't have happened."

But right in the middle of all this, something happened. The Word says, **. . . David encouraged himself in the Lord.** Right in the midst of all the distress, David said, "Wait a minute! I don't have to tolerate this! I don't have to put up with this" (Author's paraphrase).

He could have sat there, given up, and quit, but he made up his mind, "No, it's not over just because the enemy has come in and stolen my blessing. It's not over! It's never over until God says it's over! God has delivered me before and He'll deliver me again" (Author's paraphrase).

You've got to reach a point where you grow restless and make up your mind that you are not staying this way anymore and begin encouraging yourself in the Lord. Don't wait around for someone else to encourage you. There may not be anybody else. YOU have to encourage yourself! David went from distress to wanting to fight.

And David inquired at the Lord, saying, Shall I pursue after this troop? shall I overtake them? And He answered him, Pursue: for thou shalt surely overtake them, and without fail recover all.

I Samuel 30:8

When the enemy has stolen from you, not only does God want you to get up and pursue the enemy, but He wants you to literally march into His camp and recover all! God's not satisfied with you only getting up and being aggressive, He wants you to get back what was stolen.

That's exactly what David did. He pursued his enemy, he overtook them, and he recovered all! I believe the marching orders in the church today are, "Pursue, overtake, and recover all!" God is wanting an army of people to rise up and get back what has been stolen from them. Are you fed up, yet? If not, that's exactly why you're still just surviving. What you refuse to master in your life will continue to master you. Start taking action today!

4 "How can I give if there's nothing to give?"

In this chapter, I want to share with you exactly what the Lord said to me in that first visitation in October 1981.

As I was preparing to minister at the East Coast Believers' Convention in Charlotte, North Carolina, I had determined in my heart to spend a lot of time in fellowship with God. I arose even earlier than usual to be in the Word and prayer. As I shared with you earlier, Thursday of that week, the Lord supernaturally appeared to me in my hotel room. He had some vital things to share with me – vital, that is, for the whole body of Christ. As His presence filled the room, He said this to me, "My people are experiencing financial famine and I am going to reveal to you the keys that will bring them out."

Historically, every time God's people as a whole entered into bondage, the only way they were delivered was by divine intervention. In each case, God would supernaturally visit someone, and assign them to take the message to His people. I received just such an assignment from the Lord, and I am sharing that message of deliverance from financial bondage with you in this book.

When God visited me, He told me that He was going to bring about some tremendous miracles in these last days for the body of Christ where finances are concerned. However, even though He is going to divinely intervene on our behalf, there are conditions that have to be met.

How does bondage come?

Let's look at the life of Abraham, the Father of Faith. He was a godly man who completely consecrated and dedicated his life to God. Consequently, he became a very wealthy man. But Abraham never pursued these blessings. He never sought after riches and wealth. He sought God. Because his motivations were right, Jehovah Jireh, the Source of Supply and Provider of All, manifested Himself in Abraham's life. God saw to it that Abraham did not lack for anything.

On the other hand, his nephew Lot, a greedy, selfish man, was very ambitious to become wealthy. As you know, it produced bondage and Abraham had to go and rescue him from his captors.

Jacob was another who witnessed the prosperity of his grandfather, Abraham. He was about fifteen years old when Abraham died. Evidently, he did not learn very much about walking with God as Abraham had. He wanted wealth and riches, and he would do anything to get them. The Bible teaches us that God desires for His people to prosper; yet at the same time, there are strong warnings against deceitfulness, dishonesty, usury, and oppression of the poor to become wealthy. If you do not heed these warnings, the result will be bondage. Jacob had been a deceiver, and consequently, he entered into bondage.

Bondage always comes as a result of disobedience, rebellion, lethargy, and a neglect of obeying God's Word. However, if there is repentance, God will forgive you, and help you make a fresh start. When Jacob came face to face with God, he had a heart-changing experience, and began to seek God first, he was then blessed by God. The Lord even changed his name from Jacob to Israel, which means "Prince of God."

I want you to understand something that is very important. The Bible reveals to us the stories of people who failed, who made mistakes, and did things under pressure that they shouldn't have done. They missed God and got into trouble. Yet God forgave them. The moment they repented and became obedient to His laws, He would cause His blessings to come upon them. The Bible is also a story of grace, and of God's mercy and forgiveness.

God is no respecter of persons. He will also forgive you for any disobedience and then move supernaturally on your behalf to deliver you.

Why would God bless you?

And it shall come to pass, if thou shalt hearken diligently unto the voice of the Lord thy God, to

observe and to do all His commandments which I command thee this day, that the Lord thy God will set thee on high above all nations of the earth.

And all these blessings shall come on thee, and overtake thee, if thou shalt hearken unto the voice of the Lord thy God.

I want you to pay very close attention to these blessings: **Blessed shalt thou be in the city, blessed shalt thou be in the field. Blessed shall be the fruit of thy body, and the fruit of thy ground, and the fruit of thy cattle, the increase of thy kine, and the flocks of thy sheep.**

Blessed shall be thy basket and thy store. Blessed shalt thou be when thou comest in, and blessed shalt thou be when thou goest out. The Lord shall cause thine enemies that rise up against thee to be smitten before thy face: they shall come out against thee one way, and flee before thee seven ways.

Deuteronomy 28:1-7

I want you to notice what God has said here. God said that He would bless Abraham and his seed if they were obedient to His Word. Look closely at verse 8: **The Lord shall command the blessing upon thee in thy storehouses, and in all that thou settest thine hand unto; and He shall bless thee in the land which the Lord thy God giveth thee.**

The Lord said this to me, "I want to command My blessing upon My people. When I release my words upon their finances, it carries as much power as when I said, 'Let there be light!'"

I don't know about you, but I want God talking to my finances and not the world. I won't allow the evening news to dictate what is going to happen to me financially. I am in this world, but I am not of it.

Covenant people should live better than the world lives. We do not have to be depressed, oppressed, or suppressed. God has told us that He wants us to be the head and not the tail, above and not beneath. Our affairs do not have to be ordered about by this world.

If you believe what the devil says about your finances and if you believe what the news media and carnally minded people say, then those signs will follow your finances. The wisdom of the world tells us there is inflation and recession, and that you cannot overcome it. If you are convinced of this, you will never have enough. Signs will follow what you believe.

Let God's word be final authority

The Lord said to me, "I want My people to quit listening to what the world's wisdom has to say about their finances and start listening to what I've got to say about it. I am going to command a blessing upon them in order to deliver them out of bondage."

I read every scripture in God's Word where He commanded something to happen. In Genesis, chapter 1, the Spirit of God was moving across the face of the waters and God said, **"Let there be light."** And there was light. You'll find that every time God created something in the book of Genesis, it is always prefaced with **"And God said."** God said, and it was so. God told me, "I want to command a blessing upon you. All I would have to do to change your entire financial situation is say 'Prosperity Come! Lack, Go!' That is all it would take."

God calls those things that be not as though they are (Romans 4:17). The word **calleth** means to summons. All God has to do to change any situation is to say the Word. There is nothing more powerful than God's Word. It is superior to everything that is made, since all things were made by Him (Colossians 1:16). God told me, "I want to command My blessing upon my people. When I release My words upon their finances, it carries as much power as when I said, 'Let there be light!'"

Did you know that God has been talking about our finances for a long time? He has already said that He desires that we prosper and be in health even as our soul prospers (3 John 2). He has already said that He delights in the prosperity of His servants (Psalm 35:27). Where we've missed it is that we've listened to the world too long. Now it's time that we stop listening to the world, stop listening to the news media, and stop listening to anything that is contrary to God's Word. God has said that He will command a blessing upon us.

. . . For He commanded, and they were created.
. . . he hath made a decree which shall not pass.

Psalm 148:5-6

When God makes a decree, it shall not pass. In other words, it cannot be negated. When God talks to your finances, Satan cannot stop it from coming to pass.

How powerful is God's commandment?

Thus saith the Lord, where is the bill of your mother's divorcement, whom I have put away? Or which of my creditors is it to whom I have sold you? Behold, for your iniquities have ye sold yourselves, and for your transgressions is your mother put away.

Isaiah 50:1

In other words, He is telling them that their rebellion and disobedience have put them into bondage, not Him.

Wherefore, when I came, was there no man? When I called, was there none to answer? Is my hand shortened at all, that it cannot redeem? or have I no power to deliver? ...

Isaiah 50:2

Do you believe that God can redeem your finances? His Word says His hand is not shortened. **Have I no power to deliver?** Now I want you to notice how God connects redemption and the power of words.

Behold, at my rebuke I dry up the sea, I make the rivers a wilderness: their fish stinketh, because there is no water, and dieth for thirst.

Isaiah 50:2

God is saying, "I'll tell you just how powerful My words are. All I have to do is say the word and oceans, rivers, seas, lakes, ponds, streams, and creeks dry up" (Author's paraphrase). Can you imagine someone so powerful that at His rebuke, at His word, every body of water on this planet would dry up? He can do it. That's our God. That's how powerful His command is. That's how powerful His rebuke is.

Therefore, the redeemed of the Lord shall return, and come with singing unto Zion, and everlasting joy shall be upon their head: they shall obtain gladness and joy; and sorrow and mourning shall flee away.

I, even I, am he that comforteth you: who art thou, that thou shouldest be afraid of a man that shall die, and of the son of man which shall be made as grass; And forgettest the Lord thy maker, that hath stretched forth the heavens, and laid the foundations of the earth; and hast feared continually every day because of the fury of the oppressor, as if he were ready to destroy? and where is the fury of the oppressor?

Isaiah 51:11-13

Do you realize what God is saying here? He's reminding the people that their Maker, the Creator of the Universe, is still able to deliver them. God is saying, "I'm so powerful that all I have to do is say the Word and I can put your oppressor to flight. Where is your adversary, the devil? I'll take care of him!"

In righteousness shalt thou be established: thou shalt be far from oppression; for thou shalt not fear:

and from terror; for it shall not come near thee. Behold, they shall surely gather together, but not by me: whosoever shall gather together against thee shall fall for thy sake.

Behold, I have created the smith that bloweth the coals in the fire, and that bringeth forth an instrument for his work; and I have created the waster to destroy.

Isaiah 54:14-16

God is letting the people know that He created Lucifer. Originally, he was God's anointed cherub. But because of his beauty, wisdom, and exalted position, his heart was lifted up in pride and God cast him out of heaven. God is saying that since He created Lucifer, He'll be responsible for him. How will God take care of Satan? "NO WEAPON FORMED AGAINST YOU SHALL PROSPER." God says He'll see to it that no weapon formed against His children shall prosper. That's our heritage, Praise God! (Isaiah 54:17).

God is mightier than our adversary. Satan is not in God's class. All God has to do to stop the work of our adversary is speak the Word.

When God gets fed up

Bring ye all the tithes into the storehouse, that there may be meat in mine house, and prove me now herewith, saith the Lord of hosts, if I will not open you the windows of heaven, and pour you out a blessing,

that there shall not be room enough to receive it. And I will rebuke the devourer for your sakes . . .

Malachi 3:10-11a

Now notice here, that God says He will rebuke the devourer. In the New Testament, **we** are instructed to resist the devil. **We** are instructed to fight the good fight of faith. **We** are instructed to bind our adversary. The word **rebuke** means *to address sharply, reprimand, to force back.* When you rebuke the devil, you'll notice a boldness that will come upon you. As we discussed in the previous chapter, when you're fed up with the devil and finally get mad at him and rebuke him, then you become a different person. When you're fed up and mad enough to rebuke the devil, he'll leave you alone.

Well, I've got good news for you. God's fed up with the devil controlling your finances. He's fed up with hearing His children say, "I'd love to give more, but I can't." He's fed up with your not being able to give. He's fed up with His ministers not being able to build their churches. He's fed up, and He is going to rebuke our adversary.

It will take enormous amounts of money for us to do in the earth what needs to be done for Jesus to return. God said to me, "I'm going to command my blessing upon my people, for it is they who shall finance the greatest revival that has ever come upon this planet. I will do a work in their finances and I will cause them to prosper for the gospel's sake."

What happened to all your money?

God is going to rebuke the devourer for your sake. The word **devour** means *to swallow up, to consume.* That is exactly what has been happening to our finances. Have you ever had all of your paycheck spent before you could even get it to the bank? If so, then it was consumed. Have you ever had your money just seem to disappear and you wondered what happened to it all? It was swallowed up.

God is saying, "I will rebuke the one who is swallowing up your money. I will address him sharply." When the Creator of the universe speaks, the Bible says His voice is like thunder. The Bible speaks of the voice of Jesus in the book of Revelation and says it was the sound of many waters (Revelation 1:15). God's voice is a powerful voice and His words carry tremendous power. It is a frightening sound to our adversary.

God is going to speak to your finances. In the spirit realm, there will be a thundering voice heard and Satan and his forces will rock and reel under the blow of God's voice.

What should you do?

I asked the Lord what we should do. He said, "My people are in financial famine and I want them out. If they'll do what Isaac did when he was in famine, I'll reward them as I did Isaac."

And there was a famine in the land, beside the first famine that was in the days of Abraham ...

Genesis 26:1

There was a famine in that land. There is a financial famine in our land today. There is drought and lack. God pointed this out to me and said, "There was a famine in Isaac's day and Isaac obeyed me in the midst of that famine. If my people will obey me today in the midst of their financial famine, then I will command the blessing upon them. I will rebuke the devourer for their sake, and I will reward them with the rewards of Isaac."

Look at verse 12: **Then Isaac sowed in that land, and received in the same year an hundredfold: and the Lord blessed him.**

What did Isaac do? He sowed in famine and the Lord rewarded him greatly.

In Mark 10:29-30, Jesus said, **. . . There is no man that hath left house, or brethren, or sisters, or father, or mother, or wife, or children, or lands, for my sake, and the gospel's. But he shall receive an hundredfold now in this time . . .**

Here in Genesis 26:12, God didn't say the return would come in a lifetime, but IN THE SAME YEAR! I said, "God, do You mean that You want me to tell Your people to sow in famine?" He said, "Yes. The worst thing they could do in financial famine is to hold on to what little they've got. The worst thing they could do when it seems there isn't enough is to become stingy, selfish, and greedy. Tell them to sow in famine and I will reward them just as I did Isaac." God will say, "Blessings be on their finances. Devourer, get out of their finances."

Get out of bondage now

God needs for us to get out of financial bondage now. Jesus is coming soon. There is much work yet to be done, but we can do it. With men it is impossible, but with God it is possible. Satan cannot stop the preaching of the Gospel. He will try to by keeping the body of Christ in financial bondage. But God is not going to allow it, if we'll obey His voice. If you will determine in your heart to be set free, then God will move supernaturally on your finances and deliver you.

How I sowed in famine

When God revealed these things to me in October 1981, we had tremendous needs in our ministry. We were building, expanding, and more and more money was needed. We had to keep our faith on the job continuously. I had gotten to the place where I was fed up with the devil controlling my finances. God said He would command His blessings upon me, rebuke the devourer for my sake, and bring to me the hundredfold return in the same year. My wife and I agreed in the Name of Jesus that we would sow in famine, and God would give us the hundredfold return in the same year. We wrote out ten checks of $1,000 each for each of the ten major areas of our ministry: the Bible Training Center, the Christian School, the Evangelistic Association, the Radio and Television Outreach, and so forth.

I needed a bigger and faster airplane to travel to all our meetings. So we also sowed $1,000 from that account. Carolyn and I sowed $1,000 personally as well. Altogether, checks totaling $11,000 were written. In the natural, it looked foolish to give away $11,000. But God had told me, "You sow in famine and I will command my blessing upon you." We wrote out the checks and sowed them into the ministry to which God had instructed us. The same day, we received a check for $10,000!

The next week, I was given a $150,000 airplane! It was given to me debt free! In that same week, a person gave me a check for $100,000 for my Evangelistic Outreach! In one week, over a quarter of a million dollars came to us in financial miracles and before the year was over, we had received the hundredfold.

Do you know why these blessings came upon me? God *commanded* His blessing upon me and *rebuked* the devourer for my sake.

Your attitude is important

God wants to prosper His people. It is not His intention, however, for this wealth to be spent on our own lusts or to gratify our flesh. This is to finance the revival that is coming on this planet. But where will God get the money? There is a scripture that is beginning to be fulfilled on our behalf. It says that the wealth of the sinner is laid up for the just (Proverbs 13:22). The Amplified Bible says that it will eventually find its way into their hands. The world is no longer going to be a reservoir for Satan to withhold money that belongs to the body of Christ.

The way we sow in famine is also important to God. Let's look at the way people were instructed to bring an offering in Exodus 35:4:

And Moses spake unto all the congregation of the children of Israel, saying, This is the thing which the Lord commanded, saying, Take ye from among you an offering unto the Lord: whosoever is of a WILLING HEART, let him bring it, an offering of the Lord ...

In verse 10 it says, **And every wisehearted among you shall come ...** Wisehearted people are people who obey God.

Verses 21-22 say, **And they came, every one whose heart stirred him up, and every one whom his spirit made willing, and they brought the Lord's offering to the work of the tabernacle of the congregation, and for all His service, and for the holy garments. And they came, both men and women, as many as were willing hearted, and brought bracelets, and earrings, and rings, and tablets, all jewels of gold ...** Notice their attitude! They were willing to obey God.

In chapter 36, verse 3, we see that Moses received the offering the children of Israel brought. They were being obedient to the word of the prophet. Finally in verse 5 it says, **And they spake unto Moses, saying, The people bring MUCH MORE THAN ENOUGH for the service of the work, which the Lord commanded to make.**

Moses had to give another commandment in verse 6,

... Let neither man nor woman make any more work for the offering of the sanctuary. So the people were restrained from bringing.

These people were so willing to obey God that they gave more than enough. They weren't selfish but gracious, and God was well pleased with them.

In verse 7 it says, **For the stuff they had was sufficient for all the work to make it, and too much.**

Don't ever say that you don't have anything to give. You do. You have stuff! All God wants is for you to be willing to give what you have and He'll bless it back to you over and over again.

If you continue reading on into chapter 40, you'll see that the day Moses entered the Tabernacle, the glory of the Lord filled the place. From that point on, the Lord covered them with a cloud, and everywhere they went they were protected. They enjoyed divine health and divine prosperity.

If you are obedient to God and sow in famine, then He will speak to your finances. Once again, He'll do it with just as much power as when He said, "Let there be light," He's going to say, "Prosperity, come." Satan cannot stop the return from coming into your hands if you are obedient to God's Word.

In Deuteronomy 28, God commands blessings upon those who obey Him. Victory will come. God is rebuking the devourer and commanding the blessing of Isaac upon all who are obedient to sow in famine. Sow your seed and keep on sowing and watch God move supernaturally on your behalf.

PART
2
The Second Visitation

1 What to do when you're under pressure

In November 1992, as I was preaching with Brother Kenneth Copeland in the International Believers' Convention in Bournemouth, England, I received my second supernatural visitation of the Lord. Again, He visited my hotel room. In that visitation, He said some very powerful things to me and gave me a mandate to tell them to the body of Christ.

He said, *"I am holding you responsible to challenge the body of Christ to get out of survival mentality and begin to believe Me for supernatural increase and restoration."* He said, *"If you don't preach this, I will raise up someone who will."*

At the time the Lord spoke to me concerning this, because of my disobedience, our ministry had been going through the toughest five years financially we had ever known. Satan had stolen from us time and time again and we were constantly believing God for financial miracles. We were barely surviving.

I had relaxed my teaching on sowing in famine to an extent,

due to the various scandals that had taken place in some Ministries. I told the Lord that I would put those sermons "on the shelf" until everything "cooled down a little bit." Well, that was Jerry's plan – not God's. Because of that decision, our ministry went through more financial crises in five years than in the entire history of the ministry.

Therefore, when I received this supernatural visitation, in response to the Lord, I quickly said, "I don't want someone else doing my job. I'll preach it." I said, "I don't care what people think. I don't care what the media thinks. I don't care what the press thinks. I am not going to disobey You. I will preach 'Supernatural Increase' everywhere I go."

I also said, "I'm asking You for two things. Number one: I'm asking for supernatural increase to be manifested in my own life and ministry to validate the message. And Number two: I'm asking for supernatural increase to be manifested in the lives of enough people who hear me preach this to prove that I'm not an isolated case."

The Lord granted both of my requests.

We have received thousands of testimonies from all over the world of people who are experiencing supernatural increase in their lives. We have received testimonies from people who have experienced debt cancellation on their homes, properties, and businesses. We've even received testimonies from children who are experiencing supernatural increase. God is no respecter of persons – He blesses those who are faithful.

The Lord instructed me to make a list of everything the devil had stolen from us personally and from our ministry. Carolyn and I sat down and wrote out a list of everything. Under the direction of the Holy Spirit, we told the devil, "No more! You're not taking anything else from this family, from this household, from this ministry, from our children. You have stolen the last thing you'll ever steal from the Savelles. We're coming after you and we're going to recover all."

I am thrilled to report that we have checked off everything on that list. God restored in one year what Satan had stolen over a five-year period.

These are the days of supernatural increase and restoration. Increase is in the air and God gave me this mandate to preach this everywhere I go. So in obedience to God and under the direction of the Holy Spirit, I believe that this book will answer some questions you may have, and give revelation knowledge to you concerning your privileges as a child of God, as well as teach you how to get in position to receive supernatural increase in **your** life.

Have you ever awakened in the morning with a smile on your face, feeling great, looking forward to the day ahead and **suddenly** all of hell's power breaks loose? Or you're driving down the freeway, your car seems to be running great and **suddenly** everything falls out from under it?

When are you most vulnerable?

Have you ever been in a situation like that where a storm arises out of nowhere? Your child's tuition check has increased.

Your electric bill went up. Your spouse suddenly decides they are no longer happy in the marriage. You go to the doctor for a routine check up and discover you have a disease. That's the way the devil operates. He loves to catch you off guard. He is hoping that this unexpected attack will cause you to panic and you'll be unprepared to deal with it. When people panic, they throw all their Bible lessons out the window, and they respond in fear rather than in faith.

We see an example of this in Mark 4 of Jesus teaching His disciples a parable of how the Kingdom of God operates.

...Know ye not this parable? and how then will ye know all parables? The sower soweth the word. And these are they by the way side, where the word is sown; but when they have heard, Satan cometh immediately, and taketh away the word that was sown in their hearts. And when they were alone, he expounded all things to his disciples.

Mark 4:13-15,34

Jesus had just revealed to His disciples the principles of sowing and reaping. He explicitly said that once the Word is sown, Satan will come immediately to take it away; therefore, we must be on guard at all times to resist Satan's attacks. If anybody should have had a revelation of this principle, it should have been the disciples, right? I mean, Jesus Christ Himself had just expounded all things to them.

Notice what happens:

And the same day, when the even was come, he saith unto them, Let us pass over unto the other side.

And there arose a great storm of wind, and the waves beat into the ship, so that it was now full.

Mark 4:35,37

Now, when Jesus said, **Let us pass over unto the other side**, there was not a cloud in the sky. There was not even a forecast of a storm coming.

...And there arose a great storm.

The literal Greek meaning for the word **arose** is unexpected. They had no idea that a storm was coming. This thing came out of nowhere.

In the Greek, the word **great** comes from the word **MEGA** meaning *enormous, huge, overwhelming*. In other words, this storm was designed by the forces of hell to destroy them. It's MEGA. The Amplified Bible says, **...a furious storm of wind [of hurricane proportions] arose ...**

This was not just a little wind blowing, it was so great and severe that it was beating against the ship, water was in the boat and those men were frightened. Peter, James, and John were fishermen. They had been on boats all of their lives, but evidently, this storm was so bad that it caused fear to arise on the inside of them! When fear arose, they forgot everything they had just been taught. Exactly what Satan was hoping!

I've learned that Satan loves to catch us off guard particularly right after a major victory in our lives. Why? Because there's a tendency to drop your guard spiritually after a victory.

When you've been believing God for six months for something and you finally win, there's a tendency to want to take all that armor off and throw it in the closet and hope you don't have to use your faith for at least another six months. That's when you become most vulnerable to a "storm."

While you're enjoying your victory, the devil is scheming and plotting another attack. After every victory, I say, "Hallelujah!" and then I get back on guard! Don't dare throw your shield of faith off. Don't dare throw your sword down! Stay on guard!

Jesus fully intended for those men to get Him to the other side. It didn't matter if the weather was clear or a storm was raging, He wanted them to take the Word and get Him to the other side! But, the disciples panicked.

And he (Jesus) **was in the hinder part of the ship, asleep on a pillow: and they awake him, and say unto him, Master, carest thou not that we perish?**

Mark 4:38

They were so frightened to the point that they thought Jesus didn't care. That is exactly what the devil will try to tell you. He'll even send some nice Christian to tell you, "Well, if this faith stuff really works, where's God when you need Him?" Listen, if anybody cares about your livelihood, it's Jesus, so don't pay any attention to what others say.

The fact that Jesus was asleep on the ship during a MEGA storm indicates to me that as far as He was concerned, everything was under control. He obviously wasn't too worried about it. And you shouldn't be either. It may not look like it, but God has everything under control.

You and I have experienced situations like this, not necessarily out on the sea, but that's the way it seems when Satan attacks your finances, your family, your business, your church. Sometimes the attacks come in hurricane proportions and you're thinking, "Dear God, what did I do? What brought this on?"

Have you ever unexpectedly had a need for thousands of dollars before the end of the week? I have, and it's not comfortable. But God came through with a mega miracle!

Wake up!

Isn't it amazing that Jesus was **sleeping** during a mega storm! That ship was being tossed to and fro, there was water in the boat, surely it was splashing over on Jesus, but He was still asleep. They had to wake Him up.

When was the last time you slept through a storm? I'm talking about everything is coming against you in your life and yet you go to bed with the peace of God, wake up with the joy of the Lord and somebody says to you, "Wow! Wasn't that a storm!" And you say, "We had a storm?"

That's the way Jesus treated it, and He expected His disciples to use the Word and combat this unexpected storm. Notice what the next powerful line says:

...AND HE AROSE ...

The same Greek word as the first **arose**: the storm arose *unexpectedly*, and Jesus arose *unexpectedly*!

In the mega storms of life, the devil is not counting on Jesus getting you out of this storm. Just as unexpectedly as this storm arose in your life, Jesus, to Satan's surprise, will unexpectedly rise up to counter it! Hallelujah!

What did Jesus do? He REBUKED it! The Bible says that at His rebuke, mountains melt (Matthew 8:26).

And he arose, and rebuked the wind and said unto the sea, Peace, be still. And the wind ceased, and there was a <u>great</u> calm.

Mark 4:39

The same Greek word for **great** is *MEGA*.

The Amplified Bible says, **And he arose and rebuked the wind and said to the sea, Hush, now! ...**

That's all it took!

...And the wind ceased (sank to rest as if exhausted by its beating) and there was [immediately] a great calm (a perfect peacefulness).

Mark 4:39
The Amplified Bible

All it took to defeat this unexpected mega storm of hurricane proportions was the rebuke from the Word of God.

I want you to know that if you're in a storm today and your ship is being tossed to and fro and it looks like there is no way that you could possibly endure it any longer, then just remember, the Captain of your salvation has not jumped ship! He's still in your ship and He's got it fully under control!

I know what I'm talking about; I've been there! God wants you to get out of this "survival mentality" where you just hope, if anything, you come out of the storm alive. That's not God's best for your life. It's time for you to think bigger than you've ever thought before. Expect God to move on your behalf. Expect mega miracles in your life. Out of every mega storm comes a mega miracle!

You can't just wish for things to change. You can't just think about things changing. You have to put the sword of the spirit in your mouth and do exactly what Jesus did ... speak against it! Use the weapons God has given you to defeat the adversary. Everything God created was created with the words of His mouth; therefore, Satan himself is subject to God's Word.

When Jesus was tempted by Satan in the wilderness, He defeated him with the words of His mouth ... by speaking the Word of God. He consistently said, "It is written ..." You need to do the same thing. Take the Word of God and speak it out of your mouth. Speak to that storm. Speak to those finances. Speak to that marital problem. Speak to that sickness. Speak to that rebellion in your children. Don't passively accept what

Satan has done in your life. Go against him with the sword of your spirit . . . the Word of God!

From nothing to mega!

In Luke 5, we read of Peter, James, and John who were in the fishing business. They had been out fishing all night. They were in the boat for hours and hadn't caught a single fish. They had nothing to show for all their hours out on the water.

But notice what happens when Jesus came on the scene.

. . . Launch out into the deep, and let down your nets for a draught. And Simon answering said unto him, Master, we have toiled all the night, and have taken nothing: nevertheless at thy word I will let down the net. And when they had this done, they inclosed a great multitude of fishes: and their net brake.

Luke 5:4-6

In other words, a few hours ago they had nothing, but now they have MEGA. One moment you have absolutely nothing in your bank account and suddenly, you have MEGA. Could you handle that?

You've been believing God, tithing, giving, and SUDDENLY, even though it's been months, the financial breakthrough comes. One moment you had nothing, and the next moment you have more than enough. That's the God we serve. He can take you from nothing to mega.

I want you to notice what Jesus told Peter to do: **let down your nets . . .** But what did Peter really do? He let down **THE** net. What am I saying? Peter didn't fully obey. Even though Jesus blessed him, just think how much more would have been taken if he'd fully obeyed.

God gave a mega miracle to a man who had nothing. God is taking faithful people who seem to have nothing and giving them mega! If you've been faithful, then your due season is coming!

I don't know what kind of storm you may have experienced in the last few days, weeks, or months, but Jesus is in your ship and if you'll dare stand on the Word of God, then God is capable of bringing a mega calm into your life.

If you've been waking up in the morning thinking, "Dear God, I can't face another day, this is too overwhelming," keep standing on the Word of God! Keep standing. Keep standing. Keep standing. Keep confessing the Word over and over and over and over. When you think you can't confess anymore, keep confessing. Your labor is not in vain. And there will come a "suddenly" in your life. This unexpected storm will turn around and God will give you the greatest victory that you've ever experienced!

In every overwhelming experience you're facing, don't give up, don't quit, and don't get discouraged! It's time to pick yourself up, rebuke Satan and declare that there is coming a MEGA calm in your life in Jesus' Name! Remember this: **Out of a MEGA storm comes a MEGA calm!**

You have to ask yourself, "Am I willing to wait for it?" As devastating as the attack is, as overwhelming as the attack is, God can turn it around. He can turn it to the point where it is beyond anything that you can comprehend.

God's answer to great battles is great victories! God's answer to great financial attacks is great financial miracles! If this will work on wind, then it has to work on dollars. If out of a great storm can come a great calm, then out of a great financial attack, can come a great financial miracle!!! In fact, if you are in a financial attack right now and it is so overwhelming and so devastating, then you know as well as I do, if you are going to be delivered from that attack, then it's going to have to be big.

If you're saying, "This is the greatest financial attack I've ever had," then what you're saying is the miracle you are headed for is going to be the greatest financial miracle you have ever experienced!! I mean, you can't have something less than the attack! It's got to be equal to or greater than the attack. And I've got news for you. Jesus is standing up in your ship right now joining with your faith. He's rebuking the wind right along with you and He's calling for a great calm. A mega calm!!!

God wants us to believe Him for mega results. This is a time of increase, but it has to start in your own thinking. If you're going to experience increase outwardly, then you're going to have to experience it inwardly first of all. You're going to have to change your thinking where increase is concerned. You're going to have to think bigger than you have in the past.

Don't limit God by thinking in terms of just barely getting by. Don't limit God by saying, "I just hope to survive this." No, get out of that survival mode and get into increase mode. The great Provider is in your ship and He wants to bring mega miracles into your life.

Great is our Lord, and of great power . . .

Psalm 147:5

God is already great and He already has the power! He's not going to get any greater because of anything you do. However, you are affected by it as you change your thinking regarding your circumstances, and as you change your thinking regarding the greatness of God.

Your problem is not greater than God's power. Your attack is not greater than God. Sometimes it may look that way. Sometimes it looks like it's bigger than what God is capable of doing but it's not.

Cast not away therefore your confidence, which hath great recompence of reward.

Hebrews 10:35

God promises that mega rewards are in store for those who will not cast away their faith while they are under pressure. As great as your problem may be, it can never be greater than the Greater One who resides on the inside of you.

. . . greater is he that is in you, than he that is in the world.

1 John 4:4

So it's up to you. You must become mega-minded. You must become supernatural increase-minded.

Once again, if you are in a mega storm right now, and your finances are under attack, your household is under attack, your family is under attack and the thing is so overwhelming that it looks absolutely and utterly impossible to overcome, then remember that the Greater One is on the inside of you and He always arises when great storms arise.

You are not helpless and you are not hopeless. It is not over. In fact, you are headed for a mega calm in your life. If this storm is so great that it has you up all night, unable to sleep, just get ready! You're going to spend some nights not able to sleep for all the blessings and the miracles that have come on you!!! Instead of lying there thinking, "What in the world am I going to do to get out of this?" You're going to be lying there all night praising God for how He got you out of it! God will turn the captivity!

There's a mega calm for every mega storm!

Just . . . trusting God?

Have you ever asked somebody, "Well, how are you doing?"

And they respond, "I'm just trusting God."

But they say it with tears in their eyes and their head dropping before they get it all out. It's obvious they're not trusting God. They're just repeating a religious cliché. I realize we've used the phrase for years and years, until it doesn't have quite the meaning that it should. When you're trusting God, you should be excited and say it with zeal and enthusiasm. God's not a man that He should lie. It's impossible for Him to lie. So, if God promises to deliver you – then He will!

Just as impossible as it is for God to lie, it's equally impossible for Satan to tell the truth. So, why would you want to put so much stock in what the devil says? I've heard people say, "The devil keeps telling me this and that . . ." Well, laugh! It's a lie. He can't tell the truth. You ask that same person, "What did God say about it?" And they might say, "Oh, He doesn't talk to me." How is it that they hear the devil so clearly and never hear God? Because they're spending too much time with the wrong fellow.

If Satan's been talking to you, then you can count on it, it's a lie. If he says; "The money will never come," laugh, it's a lie! "You'll never be healed." Laugh, it's a lie. What does God say? It's My will for you to prosper and be in health!

Rejoice! It's the truth.

We don't want you in the dark, friends, about how hard it was when all this came down on us in Asia province. It was so bad that we didn't think we were going to make it. We felt like we'd been sent to death row, that it was all over for us. As it turned out, it was the best thing that could have happened. Then he explains this statement. Instead of trusting in our own strength or wits to get us out of it, we were forced to trust God totally – not a bad idea since he's

the God who raises the dead!

2 Corinthians 1:8
The Message Bible

If you feel that you are at the end of your rope today, then it's really not a bad place to be. Now you're forced to trust God. There's not one thing in your life that God's not able and willing to deliver you out of. If you are at the end of your rope, don't you dare give up. God is the God of comfort. He'll provide comfort for you in your situation and not only that, when it's all said and done, you will be able to impart comfort into others who are going through similar situations.

Isn't that amazing? You, yes, you ... could be the very one encouraging others who are going through the same kind of attack that you have come out of.

Take therefore no thought for the morrow: for the morrow shall take thought for the things of itself. Sufficient unto the day is the evil thereof.

Matthew 6:34

Give your entire attention to what God is doing right now, and don't get worked up about what may or may not happen tomorrow. God will help you deal with whatever hard things come up when the time comes.

The Message Bible

Too many times we get focused on what we think God's not doing. "Where is the money? Where's my healing? When will my needs be met?" If you focus on what you think God's not doing, then you're in the arena the devil loves for you to be in. God wants you to focus on what He is doing.

"Well, I don't see anything happening."

That doesn't mean that He's not doing anything. While you're sitting right here reading this book, God's doing something on your behalf. The angels are very busy working for you. God is doing something right now behind the scenes that you are not even aware of. He's causing your due season to come to pass.

"What if nothing changes?"

It's possible that before you go to bed tonight, your due season could come. "What if it doesn't?" Then get up and trust God. "What if it doesn't come tomorrow?" Trust Him all day. "What if it doesn't come in a week?" Keep on trusting God. What else can you do? You've already tried everything else. You have nothing to lose by trusting God. You have everything to gain by trusting God.

If you're really trusting God, then it's time for you to shout and praise Him. That's what Paul meant when he said, "Rejoice in the Lord always, and again I say rejoice" (Philippians 4:4). I found out the word **rejoice** means to *shout and be vocal*, but that's not all there is to rejoicing. **Rejoice** also means *to brighten up, to spin around and to leap*. When you're under the greatest pressure, you should walk around the office or in your house, and put the biggest smile on your face, spin around and leap for joy. Soon everyone around you will get the hint, "He's under a lot of pressure – look at him." But then you'll come back rejoicing with the victory report.

The thought that motivates me is that my due season could come at any moment. You never know when it's going to show up. That's enough reason to keep standing. I would hate to think that I gave up and due season was about to manifest in the next few moments!

How many times do you suppose the angels were just about to deliver your "goods" and you got discouraged and gave up? I don't like that thought.

You're blessed when you're at the end of your rope. With less of you there is more of God and his rule. You're blessed when you feel you've lost what is most dear to you. Only then can you be embraced by the One most dear to you. You're blessed when you're content with just who you are – no more, no less. That's the moment you find yourselves proud owners of everything that can't be bought.

You're blessed when you get your inside world – your mind and heart – put right. Then you can see God in the outside world ... Not only that – count yourselves blessed every time people put you down or throw you out or speak lies about you to discredit me. What it means is that the truth is too close for comfort and they are uncomfortable. You can be glad when that happens – give a cheer, even! – for

though they don't like it, I do! And all heaven applauds ...

Matthew 5:3-12
The Message Bible

A whole lot of folks have lived this way before you, and God saw to it that they were victorious and He's no respecter of persons.

God has a way out of every situation that you may find yourself in. But you must be sensitive to the spirit of God in order to hear His instructions. If you're going to be around carnal people all the time, watch television all day, worry all day, and scratch your head trying to figure out how you're going to get out of this mess, then you're not in a position to hear the instructions of God.

Are you tired? Worn out? Burned out on religion? Come to me. Get away with me and you'll recover your life. I'll show you how to take a real rest. Walk with me and work with me – watch how I do it. Learn the unforced rhythms of grace. I won't lay anything heavy or ill-fitting on you. Keep company with me and you'll learn to live freely and lightly.

Matthew 11:28
The Message Bible

What is Jesus saying? "If you're at the end of your rope, then get away with Me." Notice He didn't say, "If you're at the end of your rope, watch more television . . ." No, He said, "Spend more time with Me" (Author's paraphrase).

When you spend time with Him, don't talk about the problem. Let Him talk. You don't have to tell God all of your problems. Everything you do is exposed to Him. He already knows what you're going through. He already knows the pressure you are under. Just get before Him and say, "I've come to get away with You. Show me what You would do in my situation."

His words are life to your spirit man. You can't overcome being overwhelmed if there's not a continual flow of God's Word in your life. If you're at the end of your rope with pressure, stress, depression, or loneliness, don't give up. This is not the time to say it's over. Don't agree with your adversary. Tie a big knot in that rope, hang on, brighten up, leap, spin around, and trust God. He will deliver you! How do I know? Because He is faithful!

Don't forget that God is on your side and He promised that no weapon formed against you will prosper!

2 How to determine your destiny

Did you know that you can determine your very own destiny? You may have been told by a teacher at one time or perhaps by your parents: "Make good choices." I've heard parents say this as their children walked out the door on their way to school. Your choices will lead you down the path to good things or to bad things in your life. Your choices are entirely up to you. On the other hand, perhaps you were never made aware of the fact that your life is in your hands. Well, the truth is that you are the one who determines the course of your life based upon the decisions you make. You determine your destiny. Let's find out how.

The Lord asked me this question one time, He said, "What was the first gift I gave to man after creating him?"

I thought, "Well, that's easy. Genesis 1:26-28 says that God gave man **dominion and authority** over the earth."

Then the Lord said, "What was the second gift I gave man?"

Well, to be very honest, I had never thought of it in terms like that, so I said, "I don't know."

He said, "If gift number one is found in verses 26 and 28, then surely if you keep reading, you'll find gift number two."

I read verse 29, and it says:

. . . Behold, I have given you every herb bearing seed . . .

Genesis 1:29

Seed is the second gift that God gave man. From the very beginning, God has envisioned man as a sower of seed. Why did God give authority first and seed second? For this reason: so man could have the authority to determine his own destiny based upon the seeds that he sows.

From the very conception of man, God saw man as a sower of seeds. Why give him seeds? Because God knows, if man is going to progress, to increase, and to better himself, he will only do it through the seeds that he sows.

It was Adam's responsibility to sow them. God did not do Adam's sowing for him. And He's not going to do your sowing for you. He has given you authority.

What did you say?

God has always wanted us to be seed sowers. How? First by our **words**.

The sower sows the Word.

Mark 4:14
The Amplified Bible

Death and life are in the power of the tongue ...

Proverbs 18:21

For by thy words thou shalt be justified, and by thy words thou shalt be condemned.

Matthew 12:37

Every thought, every deed, every word is a seed.

...Whatsoever a man soweth, that shall he also reap.

Galatians 6:7

A man's harvest in life depends entirely on what he sows.

Galatians 6:7
The Phillips Translation

Your harvest depends on what you sow ... in every area of your life. Your income is based on **your** giving not on my giving. In other words, your income does not have to be based on how the economy is doing. I didn't say you won't be tested. I didn't say that it's easy. But if you're faithful with your tithe and you are a sower of seed, then God will always provide a due season. He always does.

God set the law of seedtime and harvest in motion when He created man.

**While the earth remaineth, seedtime and har-
vest, and cold and heat, and summer and winter, and
day and night shall not cease.**

Genesis 8:22

As long as the earth remains, there's going to be seedtime
and harvest. If you stop and think about it, this entire planet
revolves around the law of seedtime and harvest. The repro-
ductive system revolves around the law of seedtime and harvest.

The Bible tells us that if you sow iniquity, you will reap iniquity. If you sow strife, then there is going to be discord around
you all the time. If you sow hate, then you'll be hated. If you
want friends, the Bible says you must first of all be friendly.
What is that? Planting seeds of friendliness.

Your whole life is centered around this law of seedtime and
harvest. In Matthew 13, the term sower is not used lightly. It
describes a person and a lifestyle. Jesus never calls someone a
sower who only plants occasionally.

If you decided to plant a little patch of tomatoes in your
backyard one day, that does not qualify you to be called a
farmer. In the same way, if you plant an offering one time, that
does not qualify you as a sower.

The reason most Christians are not experiencing increase
is because they've never become sowers. They're just Christians playing part-time farmer! They only sow when their emotions dictate it, or because it seems like the religious thing to
do.

When Jesus talked about the sower, He was talking about people who have a lifestyle of sowing. So if you're not a sower, then certainly you aren't going to experience the rewards of a sower!

I can carry a wrench around in my hand but that doesn't necessarily make me a mechanic. If somebody says, "Do you have a half-inch wrench?" And I open the trunk of my car and say, "Yeah, here's one." It's highly doubtful that they'll say, "I didn't know you were a mechanic." I don't qualify as a mechanic simply because I have a wrench.

Just because you gave a tithe one day, that doesn't make you a sower. That doesn't even make you a tither. Once again, with all that in mind, the term **sower** is not used lightly. It denotes lifestyle; not just a passing fad.

The sower is conscious of the fact that he is always sowing. He knows he's a sower. He is conscious of the fact that his thoughts, his words, his actions, his deeds, his time, his money, and everything he possesses is a seed. He is seed-minded.

Be selective where you sow

The sower is very selective about how and where he plants his seed. That is very important. He is so seed-conscious that he doesn't just throw it to the wind. He doesn't speak vainly. He keeps a guard over his vocabulary. He doesn't just throw his money to whomever screams the loudest or appeals to his emotions the most.

And he spake many things unto them in parables, saying, Behold, a sower went forth to sow; And when he sowed, some seeds fell by the way side, and the fowls came and devoured them up.

Matthew 13:3-4

Notice that this man didn't get a harvest because he didn't sow in the right ground. Just because you give money away to different places doesn't mean you are going to get maximum results. You've got to sow in fertile soil.

Deuteronomy 26 reveals to us that the reason a lot of Christians are not increasing in their finances is because they are putting it in the wrong soil.

The farmer can't stand out in the field and throw his seed up in the air, then throw some out on the highway, then take some to town and throw it out in the middle of Main Street, and then expect maximum harvest. He might say, "God, I don't understand! I'm a farmer! I planted seed!! Where is my harvest?" God's under no obligation to give this man a harvest. He sowed it in the wrong place. He has no right to be called a farmer.

...a sower went forth to sow; And when he sowed some seeds fell by the way side, and the fowls came and devoured them up: Some fell upon stony places, where they had not much earth: and forthwith they sprung up, because they had no deepness of earth.

Matthew 13:3-5

Is this man going to get a return on these seeds? No. He's sowing in the wrong place.

And when the sun was up, they were scorched; and because they had no root, they withered away. And some fell among thorns; and the thorns sprung up, and choked them.

Matthew 13:6-7

Is he going to get a return this time? No. He sowed seed, but they were sown in the wrong place.

But other fell into good ground . . .

Matthew 13:8

You ought to write in your Bible or in your notes: Be selective where I sow my seed.

In these last days, it is going to be vitally important that you be very selective about where you sow your seed. If you attend a church or receive encouragement from ministries where people are getting born-again, life is coming forth, lives are being changed, people are growing in the Lord . . . that's good ground. You plant in that. It's a good investment.

If it's planted in the right ground, watered, nurtured, and protected, then it will produce increase. And now what you have done is taken charge of your own financial future.

You'll never be without

God declares in His Word that real sowers will never be without seed.

Now he that ministereth seed to the sower both minister bread for your food, and multiply your seed sown, and increase the fruits of your righteousness.

2 Corinthians 9:10

This verse was not written to the "trier" but to the sower. God needs sowers. He wants you to have a sowing lifestyle so that He can join Himself to you and get involved in your finances, and in your future. What else did He say? He will not only minister seed to sowers, minister bread for your food but He multiplies your seed sown. He multiplies it!! That's the reason sowers always have seed to sow. Why? God's always multiplying their seed.

When I tithe, all I've done is show God that I am a good steward of what is His. That 10% is His. It wasn't mine. I haven't done anything yet with mine. It's when I give offerings out of the 90%, now we are talking about "mine." All I did with the 10% was show God that He can trust me with His money. The other 90% that is left is mine, so I give offerings out of what is mine.

What am I doing? I am taking charge of my financial future! You can take charge of your destiny! You can take charge of your financial future by becoming a sower; not a part-time farmer but a sower. And God promises that sowers will always have seed and their seed will always be multiplied.

I'll show you how far off we have been in our thinking.

Let him that stole steal no more: but rather let

him labour, working with his hands the thing which is good ...

Ephesians 4:28

He's talking about having a job. Working. The Bible says that a man who won't support his family is worse than an infidel (I Timothy 5:8). If you don't work, you don't eat. God believes in you and me working.

Verse 28 **... let him labour, working with his hands the thing which is good, that he may have ...**

When someone asks, "What do you do for a living?" We might say; "I am a teacher. I am a mechanic. I work as a teller in a bank." We tend to think that our job is what we do for a living. That's not the way God thinks.

He says, let him work so he'll have something to give! Look at it!!

... but rather let him labour, working with his hands the thing which is good that he may have to give to him that needeth.

God is saying that your job is not so you'll have a living. Your job is so that you'll have a giving. As far as God is concerned, your job is an avenue for Him to bless you with seed.

You could actually get to a point where your paycheck no longer sustains your life, as far as a living, but your paycheck becomes your giving!!! Can you imagine being so blessed that your entire paycheck is seed?

Isn't it going to be fun when your employer asks, "What are you going to do with your check this week? Car note, bills?" And you say, "No, this is my seed!"

"Say what?"

"My seed!!"

"Huh?"

"We're going to give all this away!! No, we don't live on this!! We give this!! We live on what comes back from this!"

Can you imagine that? That's why the Bible says God's thoughts are higher than our thoughts. That's the reason God wants us to increase in our thinking! The next time you see the word **sower**, remember that He's talking about someone with a lifestyle! Sowers have seed to sow and He multiplies their seed sown; thereby, allowing them to dictate and determine their own destiny, not what the press says, not what the economists say, not what the republicans or the democrats say. You are in charge of your destiny!

And don't just look at seed as only being money. You may not have any money to give right now, but you are never without the seed that will produce it. Did you catch that? When I first heard Brother Kenneth Copeland back in 1969, his messages absolutely changed my life. I wanted to give into his ministry so badly so that he could reach other "Jerry Savelles" just like me all across the world. I knew there were people just like me, barely making it, in debt, miserable ... and needed that life-changing word taught to them. I also knew it took money to reach those people.

However, I didn't even have a dollar that I could send him. But I wasn't without seed. I wrote him a letter and said, "If I had $1,000 to give into your ministry, I would send it. But I don't. I don't even have $1.00 to send right now. But I promise you this. The best seed I have to give into your ministry is my commitment to spending the first hour of my day in prayer for your ministry. And I believe that there will come a day when I will be able to sow $1,000 into your ministry."

Well, that day came. God honored what I had to give. My time. I sowed my time believing for the finances to be able to give into his ministry. God honors every seed sown. You may not have the money to give right now, but you are never without the seed that will produce it. You can sow seed in many different ways. You can bake a cake for someone and take it to their house. You can offer to clean someone's house, mow their lawn, watch their children, volunteer at the church. You can use the work of your hands to sow seed. You can make a phone call or write a letter to someone offering encouragement. You can pray for people. God honors every seed you sow and it will produce a harvest in your life. Start with what you've got and God will multiply it.

You determine your destiny by the seeds that you sow.

3 How to tell if you're ready to get out of survival mode

I'm a sports enthusiast! When I watch a football game, I don't just watch. I run, I block, I tackle, I take a shower at half time! By the time the game is over, I am absolutely worn out!

There's something that many people don't realize when they're crying over their team losing the game. It doesn't matter if you have the best quarterback in the league, if the receivers never get in position to receive, then they are not going to win the game. The quarterback can throw the ball perfectly, but if the receiver is turned around not paying attention or running the wrong way, then he's not going to catch the ball and consequently, they probably won't win the game.

Let me reveal this to you: there is nothing wrong with God. The problem is His people aren't in position to receive. If God's passing *increase*, if God's passing *restoration*, if God's passing *blessings*, I want them in the Savelle household – so I'm getting in position. How about you?

In the right place at the right time

Did you know that God has already made provisions for your needs? Every need you have in your life is met based on your obedience to God's instructions. When you obey God without questioning or reasoning, no matter how "strange" His instructions may seem, the provision will be there to meet your need!

We see an example of this in Mark 11:2-4,7 (New American Standard).

Jesus said to His disciples, **... Go into the village opposite you, and immediately as you enter it, you will find a colt tied there, on which no one yet has ever sat; untie it and bring it here. And if anyone says to you, 'Why are you doing this?' you say, 'The Lord has need of it'; and immediately he will send it back here. And they went away and found a colt tied at the door outside in the street; and they untied it ... and they brought the colt to Jesus ...**

Notice first of all, Jesus had a need in His ministry. He needed transportation. Notice also that God had already arranged for that need to be met – there was a colt. Jesus was very specific about what He wanted: a colt that no man had ever ridden. So, as the need arose, God was a step ahead in preparing that need to be met.

Jesus gave His disciples explicit instructions and the Bible says, **they went**. Stop and think about it for a moment. If Jesus said to you, "The car you're looking for is two blocks from here on the corner, go and get it." Would you be quick to obey without hesitation? We like to analyze everything. "How will I know the car will be there when I get there?" "What color is it, God?" "What if someone is in it?" By the time we get through questioning God's instructions, we would get there too late and the car would be gone.

If the disciples had rationalized Jesus' instructions, the man with the colt would have already left. What am I saying? Being in the right place at the right time is vitally important in having a need met. God always has the provision for your needs, but we must be obedient to His instructions without analyzing or questioning Him. Your responsibility is to believe God, believe His Word, and then act on it.

We see another example in Mark 14:12,13 (New American Standard):

And on the first day of unleavened bread, when the passover lamb was being sacrificed, His disciples said to Him, "Where do You want us to go and prepare for You to eat the Passover?" And He sent two of His disciples, and said to them, "Go into the city, and a man will meet you carrying a pitcher of water; follow him."

Follow a man carrying a pitcher of water? You mean some guy just walks around town carrying a pitcher of water all day saying, "Hear ye, hear ye, I am the man with the pitcher of water in his hand. Anyone looking for me?" Don't you know the disciples were thinking, *How do we know he'll still have the pitcher in his hand when we get there? What does this guy do, stand around 24 hours a day with a water pitcher in his hand looking for disciples?*

...And the disciples went ...

Mark 14:16

It doesn't even say, "And they reasoned among themselves." That takes a lot of faith! They were obedient to the Lord's instructions and the need was met. They found the man with the pitcher in his hand and he led them to the house of the Passover dinner. They were in the right place at the right time.

Timing is everything

Once again, Jesus had a need in His ministry. He needed a place to celebrate the Passover. When the need arose, the provision for that need was already waiting for them. There was a man with a pitcher of water in his hand, waiting to meet that need, but timing was essential.

If you stand around discussing, analyzing, and trying to figure out why God wants you to do certain things, then you may miss *the guy with the pitcher in his hand.* He's not going to stand there all day waiting for you to finally decide, "Well maybe this is God and I should obey." You've got to respond without hesitation if you're going to have your needs met.

God *always has a colt that no man has ever ridden.* God always *has a man with a pitcher in his hand.* For every need that you have, there is provision! In order to be in the right place at the right time, you must fellowship with God so you can hear His instructions. Don't go around town asking everyone, "Are you the man with the pitcher in his hand?" Let God show you. He will show you. Trust Him.

My challenge for you

It's wonderful when you're in the right place at the right time, the divine connection has been made and your need is met, but I want to share with you something deeper than that. Most Christians spend their entire lives looking for the man with the pitcher in his hand, but I've got a better way of life to suggest to you today: BE THE MAN WITH THE PITCHER IN HIS HAND!

Meeting the need for somebody else is Christianity at its best! It's wonderful to receive, but it's even greater when you get to be the one blessing others.

"Oh, Brother Jerry, let's talk about getting it first, then we'll talk about giving it later."

No, that's the wrong mentality. When you start giving, God will give back to you all you can handle!

The greatest joy you'll ever know

. . . And I will bless you, And make your name

great; And so you shall be a blessing.

Genesis 12:2
New American Standard

Why does God want you blessed? So, you can be a blessing. What is a **blessing**? *An instrument through which God's divine favor flows bringing peace, joy, and happiness and preventing misfortune in the lives of others.* This is the way God wants you to live.

You can read Genesis 12:2 like this, *"I will empower you to prosper so that through your prosperity, you can bless others"* (Author's paraphrase). In reality, all you are is a clearinghouse – a distribution center. It comes to you, and goes through you. That's life at its best!

Several years ago, I went to preach at a small church in South Texas where there were only a handful of people. After the service was over and I was getting ready to drive back home, the pastor said, "Brother Jerry, we just want to bless you and Carolyn personally. Don't use it in the ministry. This is for you and Carolyn. Use it on something you and Carolyn would like." And he handed me a check for $1,000. I thought, *That's a lot of money for a handful of people to bless us with.* I didn't want to receive it, but he told me to practice what I preach and don't rob them of their blessing!

So, as I was driving home, I began thinking of all the things that I could spend that money on. I could see myself in a new leather jacket to wear on my motorcycle. In fact, the more I thought about it, I already had Carolyn's part spent. I could think of a dozen things that I could spend that money on.

When I got home, Carolyn was still awake and she said, "Oh, I'm so glad you got here before midnight." I said, "Why?" She said, "Well, there's a couple that are being evicted from their home. They've got to have $1,000 by midnight or they'll be put out of their home, and I just believe that we're supposed to help them."

I said, "I've got $1,000 right here that was given to us personally to use on whatever we want." She said, "That belongs to them. Let's get over there and keep them from having to move."

We drove to their house and saw all four of their little children carrying boxes out to the car. Everybody was packing. When we walked up, one of the children said, "Brother Jerry, what are you doing here?" I said, "Come on kids, we aren't moving tonight. Let's take it back into the house."

We moved those folks back into their home and paid the $1,000 they needed, and I want you to know that afterward that was the best night of sleep I'd had in years. The joy that we saw on those little faces who didn't have any idea where they were going . . . and the parents with tears pouring down their cheeks – nothing replaces the joy of "being the man with the pitcher in his hand."

What were we doing? Preventing misfortune in the lives of others. God allowed us to be blessed so we could be a blessing. That is the greatest joy that you will ever know in your life.

The law of increase

You may be thinking, "Well, if I'm blessed and I give it away, what about me?" Read this verse.

There is that scattereth, (or distributes) **yet increaseth;**

Proverbs 11:24

It's the law of increase. You cannot outgive God. You distribute and it creates increase. Another translation says, **it is possible to give it all away and yet become richer.**

The Bible says that the one who withholds his blessings or refuses to give will result in want or poverty. If God tells you to bless someone, then be quick to obey and bring peace, happiness, and joy into someone's life.

Which is more fun? Always looking for the man with the pitcher in his hand, or being the man with the pitcher in his hand? From here on out, never again ask God to just meet your needs. From now on say, "God, empower me to prosper!" Why? Because if all you get is your needs met, then you can't be a blessing. *Empowered to prosper* means your needs will be met and you'll have plenty left over to bless others.

Be the man with the pitcher in his hand. Get involved in blessing others and God will see to it that every desire of your heart is met far above anything you could ever ask or think. Why does God want you blessed? To be a blessing!

When you make it a lifestyle to look for opportunities to be a blessing to someone else (with whatever you have to give), THEN you're ready to get out of a survival lifestyle.

4 Four things that will stop your progress

Many, probably most, people are living from paycheck to paycheck. They aren't increasing; they are just surviving. That could be you. When God visited me and gave me this mandate to preach, He instructed me to challenge the Body of Christ to get out of this survival mentality and begin to believe Him for supernatural Increase.

You may be thinking, "That's great for you, Jerry, but how does it affect me?"

Increase is available to anyone who will dare believe for it. God's doing it! He's not doing it because it's something Jerry Savelle thought of. No, I just decided to get in the flow of it, I'm tapping into it, and God is confirming His Word with signs following. It is God's will for YOU to experience supernatural increase in every area of your life!

Before the Saints are going to be caught away, God says there are some things that must come to pass first. One of those things is, "This Gospel must be published to all the nations" (Matthew 24:14).

That states the kind of financial position that God wants the Body of Christ in. If we're going to publish the Gospel to all the nations, we must have the resources to do it. We can't publish the Gospel to the nations if we're broke! God wants us to increase!

O Israel, trust and take refuge in the Lord! (Lean on, rely on, and be confident in Him)! . . .

Psalm 115:9
The Amplified Bible

Ye that fear the Lord, trust in the Lord: he is their help and their shield. The Lord hath been mindful of us: he will bless us; he will bless the house of Israel; he will bless the house of Aaron. He will bless them that fear the Lord, both small and great. The Lord shall increase you more and more, you and your children. Ye are blessed of the Lord which made heaven and earth.

Psalm 115:11-15

Again, this is a solemn promise of God that those who fear Him and trust Him will increase more and more. God doesn't expect you to remain the same after you have entered into covenant with Him. He expects everything around you to increase. He expects you to increase in your knowledge of God, in the peace of God, and in the grace of God.

God's in the multiplying business. You never see God subtracting things from His people. If you refuse to increase, and just live in survival mode, then you're actually refusing God the right to fulfill His covenant. In other words, if you're not willing to let God increase what you're doing, then you are literally tying God's hands. In His mind, this is a covenant of increase. You can't stay the same. You can't go year after year and remain the same. God's expecting you to grow and to increase in every area of your life.

Hopefully, you're absorbing the Word that you're reading from this book and will apply it to your life. When God brings increase into your life then you can go tell somebody else so it will help them, too. That's what I'm endeavoring to do in this book. If you'll apply the principles of God's Word that I'm sharing with you, supernatural increase will come. It just will.

It wouldn't be right for me to share all of this with you without also sharing the hindrances to supernatural increase. There are things that can actually stop the blessings from coming. Let's take a look at four areas, in particular, that will stop your progress.

#1. **A lack of faith.**

The Lord showed me the illustration in Luke 5 of a time when Jesus was teaching in a house that was full of people. The Word says that as Jesus taught, the power of the Lord was present to heal. I like to say it this way, "Healing was in the air!"

However, the Bible does not record one person in that room receiving healing ... UNTIL, a man who couldn't walk was brought to the meeting on a stretcher. When his friends noticed there was no room in the house, they climbed on the roof, tore off the shingles, and lowered the man down into the presence of Jesus. At that point, the Bible says that when Jesus **saw their faith**, it was THEN that someone was affected by the healing that was already in the air.

FAITH is what made the connection! In other words, even though healing was in the air, a LACK OF FAITH could hinder you from experiencing it.

I just want you to know that supernatural increase is in the air! BUT, YOU MUST TAP INTO IT! You tap into it the same way you tap into healing, salvation, and deliverance – WITH YOUR FAITH!

#2. **Holding onto the past.**

Behold, the former things are come to pass ...
Isaiah 42:9

In other words, don't live in the past; that's already happened. It's over. Quit feeling sorry for yourself and dwelling on your past. It's time to move on!

If you've been knocked down, if you've had setbacks, it's time to get up! The most natural thing to do when you fall is get up! Don't lay there the rest of your life! One of my favorite verses is Micah 7:8 – **When I fall, I shall arise!**

What would you think if I were to walk out to a parking lot, stumble and fall and land flat on my back, and then you come along and say, "Jerry, what happened?"

I would say, "I fell."

You'd say, "Well, are you hurt?"

I'd say, "No, I don't think so."

You'd probably say, "Then, get up!"

Suppose I responded with "Well, I don't want to assume I could get up. After all, it could be the will of God that I lay here – since I fell."

That's the way a lot of people live their lives. They fall and refuse to get up. Some people even think "it was the will of God." Don't major on the fall, major on getting up!!!

It doesn't matter what kind of financial setbacks you have had in the past – it's a new day. It's time for you to look ahead and tap into the increase that's available to you.

Behold, the former things are come to pass, and new things do I declare: before they spring forth I tell you of them.

Isaiah 42:9

**Do not [earnestly] remember the former things
neither consider the things of old. Behold, I am doing a new thing! Now it springs forth; do you not per-
ceive and know it and will you not give heed to it? ...**

Isaiah 43:18-19

The Amplified Bible

God is saying that He is going to do something NEW in
your life. God doesn't want you to live in the past. How you
lost what you lost is not important now. Don't rehearse what
happened to you in the past. God wants something new to
happen in YOUR life!

#3. **The spirit of the world.**

The spirit of the world will stop supernatural increase. The
world is getting more worldly, but at the same time, the Holy
Spirit is endeavoring to get the church more Godly. You can't
be a "worldly believer" and expect supernatural increase.

How do you know if the spirit of the world may have come
into your life? Well, you can determine it by a number of scriptures. For instance, Revelation 2:4 says, **Nevertheless I have
somewhat against thee, because thou hast left thy
first love.** If you've left your first love, then that is a sign that
the spirit of the world has come into your life.

2 Timothy 3:4 says they become **... lovers of pleasures
more than lovers of God.**

If you don't have constant fellowship with the Holy Spirit

and constant union with the Word of God, then obviously, the spirit of the world is going to come into your life.

Jesus said one of the things that will choke the Word in your life is the cares of this world. There are so many things out there that pull on us to distract us. And there are many Christians who have become totally distracted – they've left their first love. They're more involved in self-gratification rather than pleasing God. And yet these same people are believing for restoration, recovery, and supernatural increase, but they've still got sin in their life and then won't do a thing about it! You cannot allow the spirit of the world to come into your life. You must have a heart that is truly after God.

#4. **Unwilling to change.**

Many times there are some adjustments that need to be made in our lives. We all must be willing to make changes. The Lord said to me, "The reason that some will not enter into this new thing (or supernatural increase) is simply because they are not willing to make the necessary changes."

Some will not experience restoration and refreshing even though it is happening all around them. There will be some who will stand by, scratching their head trying to figure out why it's not happening to them even though it's in the air. Change is vital!

In Luke 5, we see a parable concerning leaving the old and embracing the new.

But new wine must be put into fresh wineskins. And no one after drinking old wine immediately desires new wine, for he says, The old is good or better.

Luke 5:38-39

The Amplified Bible

Notice it says, **But new wine MUST . . .** The word **"must"** implies that it is imperative. We really don't have any option. This scripture is saying that not everyone will be quick to change. Some will hesitate. Some will procrastinate. Some will stand outside and see if anything is going to happen before they get in. They want more evidence.

The apostle Paul said it this way, **All things are lawful unto me, but all things are not expedient . . .** (1 Corinthians 6:12) or profitable. He's saying, "There are some things in my life that are not necessarily sinful, but they're just no longer profitable. Anything that will hinder me from being in the flow of what God's doing, then I must change that!" (Author's paraphrase). Become sensitive to change and be quick to do it!

He that covereth his sins shall not prosper: but whoso confesseth and forsaketh them shall have mercy.

Proverbs 28:13

One translation says, **he who habitually covers his sin**. In other words, that's a person who knows he's wrong and won't do a thing about it.

But for the person who confesses his sin, he's making the necessary changes. He's removing all the things in his life that are hindering him from experiencing mercy. He's making the changes and doing it quickly. And as a result, God says he is a candidate for supernatural increase!

In order to avoid the "hindrances" to supernatural increase, you must (1) use your faith, (2) let go of the past, (3) resist the spirit of the world, and (4) make the necessary changes in your life.

Concentrate on doing these things and you will be in position to receive.

5 Three things needed for supernatural increase

When the Lord supernaturally visited me in 1992 and gave me the mandate to encourage His people to get out of survival mode and into supernatural increase, I began studying illustrations and examples of people in the Bible who experienced this supernatural increase in their lives. In that study, I recognized a pattern. There are always three things needed in order for you and I to experience increase. Let's look at the example of Elijah and the widow woman.

And Elijah the Tishbite, who was of the inhabitants of Gilead, said unto Ahab, As the Lord God of Israel liveth, before whom I stand, there shall not be dew nor rain these years, but according to my word.

And the word of the Lord came unto him, saying, Get thee hence, and turn thee eastward, and hide thyself by the brook Cherith, that is before Jordan.

And it shall be, that thou shalt drink of the brook;

and I have commanded the ravens to feed thee there.

So he went and did according unto the word of the Lord: for he went and dwelt by the brook Cherith, that is before Jordan.

And the ravens brought him bread and flesh in the morning, and bread and flesh in the evening; and he drank of the brook.

And it came to pass after a while, that the brook dried up, because there had been no rain in the land.

I Kings 17: 1-7

What is God saying?

When you are experiencing lack in your life, what you desperately need first of all is **a word from the Lord**.

And the word of the Lord came unto him saying, Arise, get thee to Zarephath, which belongeth to Zidon, and dwell there: behold, I have commanded a widow woman there to sustain thee.

I Kings 17:8-9

Notice, God had already visited this woman. He had already gone ahead of Elijah. God is always a step ahead. He already has it figured out. He already knows what it will take for you to get your needs met.

God had already gone to Zidon, talked to the widow woman, and then, He told Elijah to go there and he would be sustained.

So he arose and went to Zarephath. And when he came to the gate of the city, behold, the widow woman was there gathering of sticks: and he called to her, and said, Fetch me, I pray thee, a little water in a vessel, that I may drink.

And as she was going to fetch it, he called to her, and said, Bring me, I pray thee, a morsel of bread in thine hand.

And she said, As the Lord thy God liveth, I have not a cake, but an handful of meal in a barrel, and a little oil in a cruse: and, behold, I am gathering two sticks, that I may go in and dress it for me and my son, that we may eat it, and die.

I Kings 17:10-12

I want you to notice that this woman fully intended to prepare this meal as her last meal. That was her vision; that's as far as she could see. She was going to prepare this last meal with what little bit she had left and die. But God had already visited her. Apparently, what God said to her went totally against all her natural reasoning.

God said that He had already commanded her to feed this prophet. But when the prophet showed up, she said, "I can't."

Sound like anyone you know?

When you and I argue with God because it goes against natural reasoning, then we are really saying that we are smarter than God. And the greatest revelation you will ever get is, *God is smarter than thee.*

She was saying, "You don't understand my problem. I have enough to prepare one last meal for my son and me. We are going to eat it and then die." Obviously, this woman needs supernatural increase! Now let's look at the three things that are going to bring about supernatural increase in her life.

And Elijah said unto her, Fear not; go and do as thou hast said: but make me thereof a little cake first, and bring it unto me, and after make for thee and for thy son. For thus saith the Lord God of Israel ...

I Kings 17:13

#1. **The first thing you need is a prophetic word from God.**

You need a rhema word; a word in season for you. You need a word coming directly from the throne of God. And you need to know in your heart, without any doubt whatsoever, that you have heard the voice of God.

In this illustration, we see that before there could be supernatural increase, there had to be a prophetic word.

Verse 14 – **For thus saith the Lord God of Israel ...**

Now here is the word from God: **... The barrel of meal shall not waste, neither shall the cruse of oil fail, until the day that the Lord sendeth rain upon the earth.** Those were God's Rhema Words to her regarding her needs.

#2. **Secondly, there has to be OBEDIENCE on the part of the person to whom the prophetic word is spoken.**

Once you hear the prophetic word, then you must follow it with obedience.

In verse 14 – the prophetic word: **For thus saith the Lord God of Israel, The barrel of meal shall not waste ...**

Verse 13 – the demand for obedience: **... go and do as thou hast said: but make me thereof a little cake first ...**

In other words, if she hadn't made that little cake first, then there could have been no supernatural increase. Even though, in the natural, what he was telling her to do was impossible. That's a very important point. Usually, the word from God is going to run cross grain with natural logic. For the Holy Spirit to say to you, "Touch His clothes and you'll be made whole," that doesn't agree with logic. Your mind will argue, "What's touching His clothes going to do? That's ridiculous! I can plainly see everyone is touching Him and nobody is being healed." Yes, but if that's what God told you to do, then just do it!

Don't think about it

If the little woman obeyed, then God promised that the barrel of meal would not waste, neither would the cruse of oil fail. If she had argued, "I can't do this. You don't understand. I don't have enough. I told you, Elijah. I don't have enough," then she would have been responsible for stopping supernatural increase in her life simply because she let her mind and her own reasoning get in the way of the Word of the Lord.

Verses 15-16: **And she went and did according to the saying of Elijah: and she, and he, and her house, did eat many days.**

And the barrel of meal wasted not, neither did the cruse of oil fail, according to the word of the Lord, which he spake by Elijah.

She was obedient.

#3. **The third thing you need is a point of contact which will usually require sowing a seed.**

God will always give you a point of contact for the purpose of releasing your faith. It is what I like to call, "something you can hang your faith on." It is a reference point. Just like the little woman who said, "If I but touch his garment, I shall be made whole" (Matthew 9:21). The virtue was not in His garment because if that were true, then every person who touched Him would have been healed. When she touched Him, Jesus immediately stopped and said, "Who touched Me?"

The disciples said, "Master, the people are thronging You. Everyone is touching You." But He said, "No, this is a different touch. This was the touch of faith" (Author's paraphrase). It stopped Him in His tracks. Notice it was not the clothing that made her whole. It was the establishing of a point of contact . . . touching His clothes. In other words, something she could rest her faith on. Touching Jesus' clothes was something that she focused on to release her faith and expect her miracle.

We see a "point of contact" used throughout the Word of God. Jesus used the point of contact in many different ways. Sometimes He made spittles of clay and He put the clay in a blind man's eyes. There is no virtue in clay. There is no virtue in spit. But He actually did it. He spat on the ground, made a spittle of clay, and He put it in the man's eyes. It's a good thing the man was blind. If he'd seen all this, he probably would have gotten out of the prayer line. The spittle of clay was simply a point of contact.

Notice Jesus didn't do that everywhere He went. He didn't do that to every blind person He prayed for. When He put that spittle of clay in the man's eyes, and they were opened, notice Jesus didn't turn to Judas, who was the treasurer, and say, "All right, boys. Make spit balls and put them in the treasury box. From now on, this is the way we pray for folks." No. Did you notice, He didn't say, after that little woman touched His clothes, "All right. Let's cut my robe up. I can buy a new robe. We'll sell this on the radio." No. It was simply a point of contact. It was a reference point. It gave her something on which she could release her faith.

The three things essential to supernatural increase in your life are: (1) You need to hear a word from God; (2) You must obey that word, and finally; (3) You need to establish a point of contact.

Don't just say, "Well, that's just a Bible story!" It really happened. And if the Bible is true and we believe it is, Jesus is the same yesterday, today, and forever. If you're going to believe for supernatural increase, then you're going to have to read the Bible again and recapture that childlike faith where you just believe it! Begin to get a fresh revelation of just how awesome God really is, and the unlimited ways that He has of bringing about supernatural results in our lives.

"Did I hear you correctly?"

And Jesus, when he came out, saw much people, and was moved with compassion toward them, because they were as sheep not having a shepherd: and he began to teach them many things.

And when the day was now far spent, his disciples came unto him and said, This is a desert place, and now the time is far passed:

Send them away, that they may go into the country round about, and into the villages, and buy themselves bread: for they have nothing to eat.

He answered and said unto them, (Now here comes

the word of the Lord): **Give ye them to eat. And they say unto him, Shall we go and buy two hundred penny-worth of bread, and give them to eat?**

He saith unto them, How many loaves have ye? go and see. And when they knew, they say, Five, and two fishes.

And he commanded them to make all sit down by companies upon the green grass. And they sat down in ranks, by hundreds, and by fifties.

And when he had taken the five loaves and the two fishes, he looked up to heaven, and blessed, and break the loaves, and gave them to his disciples to set before them . . .

Mark 6:34-41

Notice, the Word of the Lord: God told them exactly what to do. Then, He established the point of contact. He gave the five loaves and fishes to the disciples and instructed them in what to do with them. What would you have done if you had been one of the disciples? There were only five loaves and two fishes! The Bible says there were 5,000 men present there. That takes some serious faith! And obedience!

Do you see what I'm getting at? When God tells you to do something, it may sound strange to your natural mind. If you try to reason it out, you'll eventually talk yourself out of doing it altogether. You may even convince yourself that it wasn't even God talking to you. You'll think it was just your own voice or maybe even the devil.

Don't reason everything out. I like to say, "Be quick to obey!" I always told my two daughters when they were growing up, "Obey quickly and quietly." I learned that lesson from God. Don't question. Don't argue. Don't reason. Obey His voice quickly and quietly.

And when He had taken the five loaves and the two fishes, he looked up to heaven, and blessed, and brake the loaves, and gave them to his disciples to set before them; and the two fishes divided he among them all.

And they did all eat, and were filled. And they took up twelve baskets full of the fragments, and of the fishes. And they that did eat of the loaves were about five thousand men.

Mark 6:41-44

God is the God of supernatural increase. Only God can make something impossible possible. And again, He is no respecter of persons. Throughout the Bible, you will see God blessing people supernaturally over and over. In what looks to be the most impossible situation, God can drastically turn it around. These are not just Bible stories. They were written as encouragements for us to base our faith on. They serve as reminders of the God we serve ... the God of the increase.

Notice what had to come before the supernatural increase could be manifest:

#1. **The word of the Lord.**

What is God saying in your situation? What you're reading right now could be the Word of the Lord for you today. If you are in lack, then you need to hear from God. If you need a miracle, then first of all, you need to hear from God. If it's impossible for you to pay your bills, then you need a Word from the Lord. If your situations look impossible, then you need a rhema from God – a word from the Lord. Stay in a position to hear that word.

#2. **Obedience.**

Be quick to obey what God tells you to do. If you're going to have supernatural increase, then you must do exactly what He instructs you to do ... the way He said to do it. Don't alter it.

#3. **Establish a point of contact whereby you can release your faith.**

Declare that the moment you establish your point of contact. That's the moment you believe you have received. It has already happened in the spirit realm, and now it needs to manifest in the natural realm. Regardless of what your mind says, regardless of what your circumstances say, release your faith and expect your breakthrough.

Even if two weeks have gone by. You look back to that reference point and say, "No, that's when it happened, in the Name of Jesus! That's when I released my faith. Thank You,

Lord, that it's in Your hands and You will perfect that which con-
cerns me!"

What will be the results? Supernatural increase and
restoration. Now lay hold upon this revelation and watch it
drastically change your life, your family, your finances and your
ministry.

If God can do it for me, He can do it for you.

PART
3
The Third Visitation

1 "Is there some kind of curse on my life?"

In Part 3 of this book, I want to share with you the messages leading up to that third visitation in Liberty, Texas. I received some of the most life-changing revelations from the Lord preceding that visitation that put my life and ministry into position for some of the greatest breakthroughs that I have ever experienced. God is so awesome. He shared some truths with me that I want to reveal to you that I believe will drastically change your thinking and your present circumstances just like they have mine.

Let me ask you. Does it seem that no matter how hard you work at something, it doesn't seem to ever change? Does it feel like the blessings of God have stopped? What is it? You're in a rut, so-to-speak and something needs to change.

There have often been times that my blessings have been blocked. My quest was to discover what caused it. What is blocking my blessings? If we can discover scripturally what is blocking our blessings, and why we've found ourselves in a rut, then we can correct it. We can make the necessary adjustments, and then the blessings will flow again.

I want to share with you something very powerful that the Lord showed me about my own life and ministry. When I received this revelation and then applied it to my situation, things began to change. The change was not prolonged either. In some cases, I experienced breakthrough within 24 hours. God reversed some situations in my life and brought breakthrough in areas where we had been struggling for several years. He is the God of the breakthrough and I believe that if you'll grasp what He shared with me, it will change your life, too.

And it shall come to pass, if thou shalt hearken diligently unto the voice of the Lord thy God, to observe and to do all his commandments which I command thee this day, that the Lord thy God will set thee on high above all nations of the earth: And all these blessings shall come on thee, and overtake thee, if thou shalt hearken unto the voice of the Lord thy God.

Deuteronomy 28:1-2

If you continue to read, it becomes obvious that God wants to bless us in every area of our lives. He wants to bless us financially, physically, mentally, and socially. But notice there is a condition – "If you will hearken diligently unto the voice of the Lord thy God and obey."

As we discussed in the previous chapter, obedience brings the blessing into your life. Now let's see what disobedience will bring?

But it shall come to pass, if thou wilt not hearken unto the voice of the Lord thy God, to observe to do all his commandments and his statutes which I command thee this day; that all these curses shall come upon thee ...

Deuteronomy 28:15

You read it. I didn't come up with this verse. We clearly see that obedience opens the door to the blessings; disobedience blocks the blessings and opens the door to a curse.

As the bird by wandering, as the swallow by flying, so the curse causeless shall not come.

Proverbs 26:2

In other words, curses do not have the right to operate in your life without a cause. The New King James Version says – **A curse without a cause cannot come.** The Holy Spirit told me to refer to the curse as a "blessing blocker." Solomon makes it very clear that curses or blocked blessings cannot occur unless there is a cause for it.

Moses tells us in Deuteronomy, chapter 28, that disobedience will block your prosperity or keep you in a financial rut.

And thou shalt grope at noonday, as the blind gropeth in darkness, and thou shalt not prosper in thy ways: and thou shalt be only oppressed and spoiled evermore ...

Deuteronomy 28:29

Spoiled evermore would mean that you just gave the devil a right to steal everything you've got. He will steal

everything you have when you open the door through disobedience.

**Therefore shalt thou serve thine enemies which
the Lord shall send against thee, in hunger, and in
thirst, and in nakedness, and in want of all things ...**

Deuteronomy 28:48

If you are in a financial rut, then I would encourage you to
search your heart real quick and ask yourself where you have
been disobedient. This will require some soul-searching. You
need to find out what is blocking your blessings. Where have
you been disobedient? Ask the Holy Ghost to reveal to you
where you have missed it. I want to share with you four possible areas where you might have been disobedient, or four
ways to get out of this rut. Some of these points have been
mentioned at some point earlier on in this book; however, faith
comes by hearing and hearing and hearing! It takes a continual flow of God's Word into your heart to bring about change.

#1. **Put God first.**

Ask yourself, "Am I putting God first place in my life or
have I let things become more important to me?"

**But seek ye first the kingdom of God, and his
righteousness; and all these things shall be added
unto you.**

Matthew 6:33

God is not against us having things; He is against things having us. God wants to bless you beyond your wildest imagina-

tions. But is your primary pursuit to know Him, to fellowship with Him, to be more like Him? If God plays a secondary role in your life, then a door has been opened for Satan to come in and block God's blessings. If you are putting God first, then the door has been shut. Satan does not have the right to block your blessings. In order to put God's Word first, you may have to change some things in your present environment.

Is your home inviting?

Have you ever walked in a friend's house and without ever hearing a word, you sensed strife or an uneasiness in the atmosphere? You could just tell that something was going on. Or perhaps you've gone in a place where you knew there was sin and you just felt this stirring inside that made you feel uncomfortable? You just felt that things weren't right. What about the opposite effect? Have you ever been in a house where you felt such peace and love that it was almost tangible? You left feeling good inside.

I have experienced both, many times. I'm sure you have too.

I want you to think for a moment about the condition of your home. What would someone feel if they visited you today? Tension, pressure, stress, strife, depression, uneasiness? Or would they feel peace, quietness, love, the presence of God in your home? More than that, what would Jesus sense if He walked through your front door today?

What is the condition of your home? Is it inviting? Is it

comfortable for the Holy Spirit to reside? If it's not, then it's time to do some cleaning. It's time to set a goal to make your home welcoming to the presence of God.

As you begin to put God's Word first place in your life, you will begin to experience more of His presence in your midst. He wants you and I to experience more of His presence than ever before. So how do we do that?

Well, it certainly starts with spending quality time with God. Listen to what the Psalmist said about the presence of God in Psalm 91:1.

He that dwelleth in the secret place of the most High shall abide under the shadow of the Almighty.

Notice the key word is **dwelleth**. In other words, we're not talking about Christians who only seek God when they're in trouble. No, this should be something you are involved in every day of your life.

The Amplified version says it this way, **He who dwells, in the secret place of the Most High shall remain stable and fixed under the shadow of the Almighty [Whose power no foe can withstand].**

That is a great statement. Wouldn't you love to have stability in your finances, your job, your marriage, and your health? No matter what's happening around you, you remain stable. God promises this to the person who abides in His presence.

The Psalmist declared in Psalm 27:5-6, **For in the time of trouble he shall hide me in his pavilion: . . . And now shall mine head be lifted up above mine enemies . . .**

When you know that you're abiding in the presence of God, you don't have to worry about anything because you know God is on your side. God will see to it that no weapon formed against you shall prosper.

Verse 13 (The Message Translation) says, **I'm sure I'll see God's goodness . . .** Wouldn't you love to have the confidence that in tough times God will take care of you? Well, you can.

If you experience more of the presence of God in your life, then you're also going to experience more victories in your life. God always responds to you and me in direct proportion to our hunger. Jesus said, "Those who hunger shall be filled" (Luke 6:21). Well what about those who do not hunger? Could it be that they will remain as they are? Are you content with your life? Are you satisfied with the condition of your circumstances or do you want things to change?

Being in the presence of God is a result of desperation. You've got to desire it. That's what David meant when he said in Psalm 27:4, **One thing have I desired of the Lord. . .** (that is an amazing statement). **. . . that will I seek after; that I may dwell in the house of the Lord all the days of my life . . .**

What is David saying? "I have experienced God's presence before and I have decided that it is the most important thing in my life. The one thing I'm after more than anything else, is to be in His presence always" (Author's paraphrase). Now that's hunger. That's desperation. That's putting God first.

Moses expressed his hunger and his desperation for the presence of God when he declared in Exodus 33:18, **. . . I beseech thee, show me thy glory.** The word **beseech** means *to implore with a sense of urgency.* In other words, Moses is saying, "I've got to have this. I've got to be in Your presence. I've got to witness Your glory." Moses knew how vital the presence of God was to his success.

When mine enemies are turned back, they shall fall and perish at thy presence.

Psalm 9:3

Notice how powerful the presence of God is. In the presence of God, your enemies are turned back. They will fall and perish at the presence of God. That simply means that Satan's attacks will not succeed. They will never accomplish what they were set forth to do. That's good news!

Now obviously, spending more time with God will bring more of the presence of God into your life. Stop allowing Satan to rob you of your time with God. That's just the bottom line. You can't be so easily distracted. You've got to set time apart with God that is not to be interrupted. You need to establish that secret place, that prayer closet that Jesus talked about. You need that special place where you and God meet regularly. Determine in your heart right now that nothing is going to rob you of more time with God.

God manifests Himself if the atmosphere you create is conducive for Him. God shows up in an atmosphere that is comfortable for him.

There were times back in the early days of my ministry when I often stayed in peoples' homes. Once, a pastor and his wife got into strife while I was staying with them. You could hear everything through the walls. I thought, "This would be a good time to slip out of here!" It was uncomfortable. I didn't like being there. I wanted to leave badly.

Well God doesn't particularly like being in strife-filled atmospheres either.

The Holy "Guest"

I remember reading one time in a book where in some old English writings the term "Holy Ghost" was translated as "Holy Guest." When I saw that, it just really exploded in my spirit that the Holy Spirit is our Holy Guest.

Now if you and I would treat the Holy Spirit more like a Holy Guest, wouldn't the atmosphere in our homes be a little different? Do you think the Holy Ghost is comfortable in the midst of strife? I don't think so. Do you think you're going to experience more of the presence of God in your life if you are watching things on television that are displeasing to Him? I don't think so.

In order to experience more of the presence of God and know that you're putting Him first in everything you do, you need to make sure you are creating an atmosphere in which He is comfortable. If He is comfortable in the atmosphere that you've created, then obviously He's going to manifest His presence in a greater way on your behalf.

Do you want more of the presence of God in your life? Then perhaps it's the atmosphere that is keeping Him from it. What kind of atmosphere are you creating?

Paul teaches us in Ephesians how to create the right atmosphere between a husband and a wife and between children and parents; and even how to create an atmosphere that is conducive for God in the workplace; how employers are to treat employees and how employees are to treat employers. The whole book of Ephesians deals with this subject. What is Paul saying? Get it right and God will show up.

Determine to do your part. Create the atmosphere that is conducive for the presence of God to increase in your life. Determine to spend the quality time that is necessary now that you know how vital and essential the presence of God is if you want to experience greater success.

#2. **Live a Godly lifestyle.**

How is your lifestyle? Is it pleasing to God? Is the Holy Spirit comfortable with the way you live? Are you living a Godly lifestyle or have you accepted the world's standards for moral conduct?

. . . be holy, for I am holy.

Leviticus 11:45

Our disregard for God's standards for moral behavior has everything to do with our blessings being blocked. We can't compromise God's standards and expect the blessings to flow. We must shut every door.

Teaching us that, denying ungodliness and worldly lusts, we should live soberly, righteously, and godly, in this present world.

Titus 2:12

Examine the programs that you watch, the words of your mouth, and the kind of people that you fellowship with. God will bless those who respect His guidelines for moral living.

Consider your ways

I want to show you an example from the Word of God of a group of people who weren't experiencing God's best, and we'll see why this was happening in their lives. Let's see if you can relate.

Now therefore thus saith the Lord of host; Consider your ways and set your mind on what has come to you. You have sown much, but you have reaped little; you eat, but you do not have enough; you drink, but you do not have your fill; you clothe yourselves, but no one is warm; and he who earns wages has earned them to put them in a bag with holes in it. Thus says the Lord of hosts: <u>Consider your ways ...</u>

Haggai 1:5-7
The Amplified Bible

Please note that sowing much and reaping little is a violation of spiritual law. We've already discussed that God promises in His Word that we will reap what we sow. Then why are these people in Haggai not reaping proportionately to their sowing? God reveals in verse 5 the answer as to why this was happening – *... **consider your ways** ...* He even repeated it in verse 7, **... thus says the Lord of hosts:** *Consider your ways.*

The Amplified Bible says, **... Consider your ways, your previous and present conduct.** If you're sowing much and reaping little, then you need to stop and analyze your ways.

What is He referring to when He says **consider your ways? Ways** is defined as *course of action, methods and manners, conduct and behavior.* Do you think God's interested in our behavior? Do you think that your behavior has anything to do with whether or not spiritual laws work to your advantage? Do you suppose that you could live any ol' way that you want to and God would still cause His best to come to pass in your life? No. Your behavior has a profound effect on what kind of results you get.

You can't question whether the Word is true or not. You can't question whether God is faithful or not – consider **your** ways. God honors His Word; so obviously, it's not His fault. Who else could it be? Hmm ... oh yes, perhaps it's you and me! I know that it's highly improbable that **you** could be fouling things up, but let's just consider it.

Wrong behavior can hinder, delay, postpone, and even negate your harvest. It's bad enough that the devil is trying to

stop your harvest – why should you help him in the post-
ponement? It's time for you to consider your behavior. Look
at your ways and find out what you're doing wrong and then
correct it. Don't dwell on the fact that it's your fault, because
that will open the door to condemnation. Just repent, correct
it, and move on with God.

Out with the old

**. . . everything – and I do mean everything – con-
nected with that old way of life has to go. . . . Get rid
of it! And then take on an entirely new way of life –
a God-fashioned life, a life renewed from the inside
and working itself into your conduct as God accu-
rately reproduces his character in you. . . . Make a
clean break . . .**

Ephesians 4:22-24,31
The Message Bible

These scriptures just revealed to us a very profound
answer to cleaning up our lives. Everything that is connected
to that old way of life must go. Make a clean break from everything connected to your old way of living.

You have to totally walk away from that old, nonproductive
lifestyle. Get rid of every old bad habit. Run from temptation.
Turn away from it.

**Could it be any clearer? Our old way of life was
nailed to the Cross with Christ, a decisive end to that
sin-miserable life – no longer at sin's every beck and**

call! . . . That means you must not give sin a vote in the way you conduct your lives. Don't give it the time of day. Don't even run little errands that are connected with that old way of life . . .

Romans 6:6,12
The Message Bible

The decisive moment

The first step you have to take is decide to stop whatever it is you're doing that you know isn't pleasing God. Quit saying, "I'll stop Monday. I'll stop after the 1st of the month. I'll stop after vacation." Stop now. Stop today. Don't put your freedom off. It could cost you God's best manifesting in your life.

Make a clean break from lust. Make a clean break from perversion. Make a clean break from whatever has been a temptation in your life. God wants you totally free. What is your life worth to you?

That ye put off concerning the former conversation the old man, which is corrupt according to the deceitful lusts; And be renewed in the spirit of your mind.

Ephesians 4:22-23

Once again, the Message translation says, **everything connected to the old way of life has to go.** That sounds to me like you may need to do some cleaning. You may have to throw away some old memories. Put away all reminders of your old life. And start your new life today.

Do not bring a detestable thing into your house or you, like it, will be set apart for destruction ...

Deuteronomy 7:26
New International Version

Whatever is displeasing to God should be thrown out. Whatever tempts you to turn away from a godly lifestyle should be destroyed and done away with.

Stand fast therefore in the liberty wherewith Christ hath made us free, and be not entangled again with the yoke of bondage.

Galatians 5:1

Your lifestyle has everything to do with blessings coming on you or blessings being blocked from you. Get your life in order. Holiness is nothing more than loving what God loves and hating what God hates. Ask God to give you a supernatural hatred for the things that used to tempt you. Step by step, the Holy Spirit will strengthen you and guide you to help you clean up your life and get it right before God.

#3. **Walk in love.**

Sometimes this is a touchy subject; but a very serious one.

A new commandment I give unto you, That ye love one another; as I have loved you, that ye also love one another.

John 13:34

Are you walking in love or is there strife and unforgiveness in your heart? Your blessings are blocked when you refuse to walk in love. No matter how difficult it might seem, no matter how many layers of flesh it may peel off of you: forgive. Stay out of strife. Get rid of bitterness. It is a blessing blocker. It will keep your life in a deep rut if you don't dig it out by faith and daily choose to forgive. It's never too late to begin the process of walking in love.

Get the weeds off your seeds!

We all know the scripture in Mark 11:23-24. Most of us can probably quote these two verses from memory.

. . . whosoever shall say unto this mountain, Be thou removed, and be thou cast into the sea; and shall not doubt in his heart, but shall believe that those things which he saith shall come to pass; he shall have whatsoever he saith. Therefore I say unto you, What things soever ye desire, when ye pray, believe that ye receive them, and ye shall have them.

It would be nice if we could stop reading right there, but we can't. The next verse begins with **AND . . .** If you know anything about the English language, then you know the word **and** is a conjunction. It's used to continue a thought; therefore, we must continue reading.

And when ye stand praying, forgive, if ye have aught against any: that your Father also which is in heaven may forgive you your trespasses. But if ye do not forgive, neither will your Father which is in heaven

forgive your trespasses.

Mark 11:25-26

God is showing us right here that unforgiveness can hinder your faith and prevent your prayers from being answered. This is a perfect example of how wrong behavior can stop your harvest. I don't know about you, but I need my harvest to come on time. I don't want any delays.

Notice the Word says, **. . . If ye have aught against any . . .** I read this verse in another translation and it said, **Any person against whom you have a grudge . . .** Let's do a quick word study. What is a **grudge**? It is defined as *resentment, bitterness, and malice.* What does the word **malice** mean? **Malice** is defined as *deep-seated animosity, hostile feelings, ill-will wished upon another or bitterness.* This is getting serious.

When you hear the word **bitterness**, what do you think of? I immediately think of roots, and anything that has roots has to be dug up. If all you do is cut the top off, then you're not really dealing with the problem, you're just cutting it off at the surface. You've got to go down deep to get the roots out.

Follow peace with all men, and holiness, without which no man shall see the Lord: Looking diligently lest any man fail of the grace of God; lest any root of bitterness springing up trouble you, and thereby many be defiled.

Hebrews 12:14-15

Let's read it like this: **Follow peace with all men . . .**

lest any root of bitterness springing up trouble you . . .

God's instructions to us are: Keep peace with every man. If you don't, then a root of bitterness could spring up and trouble, who? YOU. It doesn't trouble the other person. It troubles you.

Every time I hear the phrase "shoots forth," I can't help but think of weeds. Isn't that the way weeds operate? They shoot forth so fast. I looked up the word **weeds** in the dictionary and it says – *any undesired plant that grows in abundance so as to crowd out the desired crop.*

I'm explaining all this to give you an illustration of something that happened in my life and how I dealt with it. I had sown a seed and was believing for the harvest to come. Years had gone by – still no harvest. The Lord kept saying to me, **"Get the weeds off your seeds."** I couldn't figure out what He meant by that. He just left it for me to pray over.

Well, I thought of everything in the world I could think of, and finally, I thought maybe I haven't been confessing the Word as I should. Perhaps I needed to be more aggressive. So, I did. Time went by, still no results. I said, "Lord, what's the problem here?"

He said, "Get the weeds off your seed."

I said, "Would You mind explaining to me what You mean by get the weeds off your seed?"

He said, "Read Haggai and consider your ways."

So, I read the verses and continued to meditate upon them for several days.

Well, my wife and I came out of a meeting one night, and as we were driving home, I was thinking about "get the weeds off your seed." Suddenly, it dawned on me. I had animosity against someone. I had been offended. I said, "God, that's what You're talking about." I turned to my wife immediately, and I said, "Carolyn, I know what God's been trying to tell me regarding the weeds on my seed."

I told her about the person whom I had this animosity toward and then right there in our automobile, I asked God to forgive me, cleanse me, and purge me of all the unforgiveness, animosity, and bitterness. I immediately began to feel a peace in my heart and I knew the weeds were gone! In less than 48 hours, the harvest, which had been delayed for **_years_**, began manifesting! Hallelujah!

Search your heart

If you're not receiving maximum results in your sowing, then you need to pray and search your heart to find out what could be preventing your harvest from coming. The Holy Spirit will reveal it to you.

It could be that you were offended by someone. It doesn't matter who is right or who is wrong, you simply cannot allow offenses in your life. It will deeply affect **your** harvest. Bitterness, animosity, resentment, and unforgiveness are like weeds choking your seeds.

Sometimes it's very difficult to forgive, but then you have to ask yourself – how desperate am I for maximum results? **Even if you're not in the wrong**, it's not a matter of who's right and who's wrong – it's doing the right thing. You might say, "Brother Jerry, you don't realize how badly I've been hurt. I have every right to feel this way." I understand how difficult it is to forgive and forget – especially when you are the one in the right, but you have to forgive, release it, and pray in the Spirit daily. It affects every area of your life.

When you get the weeds off your seed, then you're going to sow much and reap much. I want to encourage you to pray about your **ways**. As an act of your will, allow the Agape love (which is the God kind of love) to flow inside of you as you release all unforgiveness from your life. Don't go another day without digging up those weeds. There is too much at stake. I urge you to get on this today!

You've been on this mountain long enough . . .

I'm not taking lightly the fact that many people have been abused verbally, physically, and even sexually. It is a very traumatic experience. But the sad thing about it is that many of these people were abused at a very early age and are now grown adults, even grandparents, and they are still carrying this hurt around with them. My advice is to let it go once and for all!

Many people use these experiences as excuses as to why they cannot succeed in life. What they don't realize is that it's only hurting them; not the one who abused them. If this is you, it could be the very reason you're not blessed financially. God is saying, "Let it go. They can't pay you back for what they did to you. So, forgive them the debt and move on."

"Well, you don't know what I've been through. You don't know my past."

"If you'd gone through what I went through, Jerry, you wouldn't be so bold!"

How do you know I haven't been through a few things? I don't major on my past. I major on my future and my future is bright in God. And so is yours. I've had a few things that tried to hold me back, but I refused to major on that. Instead I'm going to major on what the Lord has done and is doing in my life.

You may not have been in control of your past, but you are in control of your future. And it's time to move forward. It's time to get over some hurdles, break some barriers, and remove bondages in your life.

The Lord our God spake unto us in Horeb, saying, Ye have dwelt long enough in this mount: Turn you, and take your journey, and go to the mount of the Amorites . . .

Deuteronomy 1:6-7

What was God saying to them? Simply this, "You've been on this mountain way too long." Sometimes God has to absolutely jerk the slack out of us in order to get us off that "mountain" and move us on to the next level with Him.

The Apostle Paul instructed Timothy, **. . . be instant in season, out of season; reprove, rebuke, exhort with all longsuffering and doctrine** (2 Timothy 4:2). Everybody wants to be exhorted, but sometimes you have to be rebuked. Sometimes we need to have reproof. Sometimes God has to get in your face and say, "You've been on this mountain long enough. Now get over it!"

You can't allow bad experiences to hold you back for the rest of your life. Satan is hoping that this painful past will distract you from ever being what God has called you to be. Your future is too valuable to allow the devil to steal it from you. God has a wonderful plan for your life.

God has a wonderful future in store for you, but you can sit around and murmur and complain and continue to be robbed of what God has for your life. It will absolutely block the blessings of God on your life.

Just as God said to the children of Israel, He is saying to you today that it is time for you to move on to the next level. He's planned some exciting things for your life – adventures in faith like you've never experienced before. This is the time to get so deeply committed to God that no one, including Satan, could possibly distract you and keep you from enjoying God's best.

Your journey of faith is not nearly over. Yes, there will be opposition. Yes, there will be adversity. Yes, there will be more tests. But thank God, He is still on your side and no weapon formed against you shall prosper. Keep moving forward!

Brethren, I count not myself to have apprehended: but this one thing I do, forgetting those things which are behind, and reaching forth unto those things which are before, I press toward the mark for the prize of the high calling of God in Christ Jesus.

Philippians 3:13-14

Forget the past. Forgive those who have hurt you. Don't block your blessings anymore. Strip yourself of every weight that is holding you back. Quit making excuses – that's a weight. Quit holding onto your past – that's a weight. Quit holding onto what people have said about you – that's a weight. You can't run this race with all those weights on you.

Wherefore seeing we also are compassed about with so great a cloud of witnesses, let us lay aside every weight, and the sin which doth so easily beset us, and let us run with patience the race that is set before us.

Hebrews 12:1

Lay aside the weight of unforgiveness. God has too much in store for you to allow the devil to rob you of it. It's a new day, so let's go to the next level and enjoy the journey.

#4. **Honor God with your tithes.**

Are you honoring God with your tithes and your offerings? If not, this could be why your blessings have been blocked.

Let's look at your giving. Be honest with yourself. Are you giving God what belongs to Him or are you "borrowing" it every now and then? Are you saying, "God, I'll pay you back. I just need to borrow the tithe this month," only to discover that now you are years behind?

The proper attitude for tithing is, set it aside first. Don't pay everybody else and then if there is anything left over, bring it to God.

. . . let every one of you lay by him in store as God hath prospered him . . .

I Corinthians 16:2

. . . put aside something and save it up as he has prospered . . .

The Amplified Bible

Get it out of your everyday usage so that you are not tempted to use it for something else. Your money will go a lot further on 90 percent than it will with you keeping 100 percent for yourself. Trust me.

If you've discovered in this chapter why the blessings of God seem to be blocked in your life, then it's time to make some changes. We have to take an inventory of our lives from time to time. Is God still first place in your life? Are you pursuing God with all of your strength, your whole being or have other things become more important to you? Be honest with yourself. Are you living a lifestyle that's pleasing to God? Are you walking in love or are you harboring strife and unforgiveness and bitterness? Are you honoring God with your tithes and offerings? Go through this checklist and be totally honest with yourself. These things could be the cause of why your blessings have been blocked. Remember, the curse cannot come without a cause. Make whatever corrections you need to make. Ask God to forgive you. Say what David said in Psalm 67:1 **– God be merciful unto us and bless us . . .**

We can ask God for forgiveness in these areas of disobedience and He will forgive us. The barriers will be removed. The cause for the curse will be removed and the blessings will flow. Go ahead. You can do it.

2 Tithing out of love instead of a command

In the messages preceding the third visitation of the Lord, the Spirit of God dealt with me about a sense of urgency for the body of Christ to get their finances in order. One of the assignments He instructed me to teach on was the subject of "tithe management." I'm sure you have heard of "time management" which is managing your time wisely. Well, now we need to be certain that we are managing our tithe wisely also . . . which has many rewards.

God began to reveal some things to me concerning tithing that I had never quite studied like this before. I believe it will open the eyes of your understanding and answer some of the questions you may have regarding tithing.

In Genesis 14, we read where Abraham had defeated the armies that had taken Lot captive and the king of Sodom went out to meet Abraham.

And Melchizedek, king of Salem brought forth

bread and wine: and he was the priest of the most high God. And he blessed him, and said, Blessed be Abram of the most high God, possessor of heaven and earth: And blessed be the most high God, which hath delivered thine enemies into thy hand.

And he gave him tithes of all. And the king of Sodom said unto Abram, Give me the persons, and take the goods to thyself. And Abram said to the king of Sodom, I have lift up mine hand unto the Lord, the most high God, the possessor of heaven and earth, That I will not take from a thread even to a shoe-latchet, and that I will not take any thing that is thine, lest thou shouldest say, I have made Abram rich.

Genesis 14:18-23

From this scripture, we can clearly see that God never intended for tithing to be a command.

"What?" You may be asking.

God never intended for tithing to be a command. You'll notice that God began to deal with Abraham in Genesis, chapter 12, but you will not find where God commanded Abraham to tithe between chapter 12 and chapter 14, which we just read.

If it wasn't a command by God, then why did Abraham tithe? He gave tithes out of love and honor and respect. When the Bible says that he lifted his hand unto God, that was an acknowledgment that God was his source. That's the reason he said to the king of Sodom, "I don't want anything you have. I don't even want a shoelace. I don't want it ever to be said that some man made Abraham rich. God is my source and God will be the only One who will ever get the credit and the glory for making Abraham rich" (Author's paraphrase).

Abraham believed what God told him in Genesis 12:2

And I will make of thee a great nation, and I will bless thee, and make thy name great; and thou shalt be a blessing.

He truly believed that God would keep His word and he had proof that God was not a man that He should lie. God had already increased him with sheep and cattle and land. He knew it was God that gave him the power to get wealth. He knew God was faithful to His Word. Out of Abraham's love, respect and honor for God, he decided to give Him tithes of all his increase. It was his decision.

God was not standing over Abraham demanding the tithe. It was Abraham's decision, keep that in mind. God wants you to honor Him with the tithe of all your increase out of your love for Him. He wants you to tithe because you have recognized, like Abraham of old, that God is your source of supply. That is what motivated Abraham. He tithed not because he had to but because he wanted to. He gave God tithes of all; he gave Melchizedek, the representative of God, tithes of all.

Melchizedek was a type of Christ. In Genesis 14:18, it says, **. . . he was the priest of the most high God.** Not only was he a priest but according to that same verse, he was the king of Salem. The word **Salem** means *peace*. He was the king of peace. In Melchizedek, we find a king and a priest like unto Jesus. Let's take a look at something in Hebrews 7 that will give us insight into how Melchizedek was a type of Christ.

In Bible interpretation, we find that very often there are types and shadows in the Old Testament of things to come in the New Testament.

FOR THIS Melchisedec, king of Salem, priest of the most high God, who met Abraham returning from the slaughter of the kings, and blessed him; To whom also Abraham gave a tenth part of all ...

Hebrews 7:1-2

Remember in Genesis 14 it said that he gave God tithes of all, and here it says that he gave a tenth part. Now, we understand the meaning of the word **tithe**. It is the tenth part of all your increase.

Recently, I had a minister come up to me and say that my ministry had been a blessing to his life. He said, "Your life of consistency and faithfulness has inspired my family and I just want to bless you. This is not for your ministry; this is for you personally." He gave me a check for $1,000. Well, immediately, I thought, "That's increase!" The first thing I did was take the tenth part of that thousand dollars and put it aside so that I could tithe it back to God wherever He so directed. I have discovered that tithing is something we should do on all of our increase, not just our paycheck.

If God is bringing increase into your life, then honor Him. The proper attitude was set forth by Abraham. God didn't make him do it; God didn't command him to do it. Abraham never thought, *"Oh I better do this or God might not make me rich."* Abraham's thinking was not, *"I better do this or he might not deliver me from my enemies."*

Abraham's decision to tithe was based on his love and respect for the God who had **delivered** him from all his enemies, Who **was** his source of supply, Who **had** met all of his needs, and Who **told** him that He would be Almighty God to him. He gave tithes out of love, honor, and respect.

I trust that as a result of reading this chapter, your attitude about tithing will change. Greater rewards will come when our attitude is right.

Most of the body of Christ today tithe out of fear of what might happen if they don't. If that's the way you tithe, then keep reading. The only chapter on tithing that most Christians know anything about is Malachi chapter 3, and frankly, I don't identify with the people in Malachi chapter 3. I identify with Abraham.

The people in Malachi chapter 3 are not my example. They were rebellious; I'm not rebellious. I'm not giving because I have to. I'm giving because I want to. I'm giving out of love and honor and respect. Tithing is not a drudgery to me. It was to the people in Malachi 3. They didn't want to because they didn't see any benefit in it. They didn't like doing it so God had to deal with them on a different level. I don't identify with them. According to Romans 4, we are to walk in the steps of our father Abraham.

Is there a pattern?

There is a law in Bible interpretation called the law of first mention. That simply means when you see God mention something for the first time, He is endeavoring to establish order. As my friend, Dick Reuben, says, "When the pattern is right, the glory falls." There's always a pattern. There's always a divine order and when people flow with divine order, the glory falls. How would you like for the glory to fall on your finances? Well, you have to get the order right, and Abraham established the right order.

The definition of **order** is a *state or condition in which everything is in its right place and functioning properly.* When you get the order right where tithing is concerned, then you're going to get the most out of tithing. That's when you begin to see those windows opening and blessings poured out upon you more than you can possibly contain. So the order is the way Abraham tithed; not the way God dealt with rebellious people in Malachi, chapter 3.

If you have children, does it bless you when your children obey you out of love and respect? Or do you like it better when they just do it because they have to? If you have a child who obeys everything you say out of love, honor, and respect and then you have this other child who does it only because they have to, which one is going to bring you more pleasure?

We're not talking about loving one more than the other. You love them both, but which one is going to bring you more joy and pleasure?

Well, God has two types of children. He loves both of them the same. One type of child only does things because he has to. Everything about them is a "I have to" or "I've got to."

Then, there's that other child who says, "You've proven thus far to know a lot more than I do and I know that You love me and I know You want the best for my life, and so out of love and respect, I will gladly live for You."

These are the kind of people God is looking for. Are you going to be one of them? I'm determined to be. I want to bring God pleasure with my attitude about my tithing. He has done so much for me and my family that I can't imagine not wanting to bless Him back. He has given me the shirt on my back, the food on my table, and the house I live in. He is responsible for all the increase in my life. There is no way I could ever deny Who has brought the increase in my life. Therefore, it's a joy for me to honor Him with my tithes and offerings.

To whom also Abraham gave a tenth part of all; first being by interpretation King of righteousness, and after that also King of Salem, which is, King of peace; Without father, without mother, without descent, having neither beginning of days, nor end of life; but made like unto the Son of God; abideth a priest continually.

Now consider how great this man was, unto

whom even the patriarch Abraham gave the tenth of the spoils (or the tenth of his increase).

Hebrews 7:2-4

We are discovering that Melchizedek was a type of Christ and there was something being established . . . order. In other words, when Abraham gave tithes to Melchizedek out of a heart of love, he set the example for the New Testament church.

Let's take it a step further. You'll find in your Bible that God preached the Gospel to Abraham. You cannot preach the Gospel and exclude Christ. It didn't say that He preached the law to him; it said He preached the Gospel to him (Galatians 3:8). In other words, two thousand years before Christ came, Abraham had heard the Gospel about Jesus. Are you with me?

Abraham saw Calvary. Now there were other patriarchs like David, who saw the crucifixion and the resurrection a thousand years before it took place and he wrote about it in the Psalms. In fact, David's description of what happened in the bowels of the earth when Jesus went to pay the penalty for mankind's transgression gave a more detailed account of it than even the eye witnesses who walked with Jesus and witnessed His death and resurrection. You can read it in Psalm 22.

Abraham was told the story of Christ two thousand years before Christ came and the Bible says that he believed it and because of it, God treated him like a righteous man. No wonder the Bible says that he is our example of faith. In other words, when you see Abraham, it is a type of a New Testament church. What you see Abraham doing is what you and I should be doing. We should be tithing out of love and respect and honor for God. You will never hear me say that tithing is a debt that you owe. Dr. Oral Roberts taught me this years ago, "Tithing is not a debt that I owe, but a seed that I sow." You're sowing a seed out of love, out of honor and out of respect.

God simply wants you to serve Him out of gladness of heart. When you truly are thankful for everything that God has done in your life, then you never feel like you have to tithe. Your attitude becomes, "I want to tithe." In fact, you begin to look for opportunities to give back to God because He's been so good to you. That's really all God has ever wanted, a people who will serve Him out of gladness of heart.

I WILL praise thee, O Lord, with my whole heart; I will show forth all thy marvellous works. I will be glad and rejoice in thee: I will sing praise to thy name, O thou most High.

Psalm 9:1-2

I will be glad and rejoice in Your mercy and steadfast love, because You have seen my affliction, You have taken note of my life's distresses, And You have not given me into the hand of the enemy . . .

Psalm 31:7-8
The Amplified Bible

Notice the Psalmist is saying that he will serve God out of gladness, not because He's made to, not because he's forced to but because God delivered him out of the hand of the enemy.

God took note of him when he was in distress, saw his affliction and didn't leave him that way.

**Serve the Lord with gladness: come before his
presence with singing . . . be thankful unto him, and
bless his name. For the Lord is good . . .**

Psalm 100:2-5

Jacob once declared in Genesis 28:22 (The Amplified Bible)
**. . . and of all [the increase of possessions] that You
give me I will give the tenth to You.**

Notice once again, God didn't command Jacob to do this.
If Isaac taught Jacob what Abraham taught him, then the order
that Abraham had established was perpetuated. Jacob was the
third generation. Jacob was saying that he would surely give
God the tenth. Later, Jacob testifies of the goodness of God in
his life and he makes this statement in Genesis 33:11 from the
Amplified Bible:

**. . . for God has dealt graciously with me and I have
everything . . .**

The King James says, **. . . I have enough.**

That's how good God was to Jacob. Do you suppose his
attitude toward God had anything to do with him getting into
that kind of position? Do you suppose his desire to give God
the tenth out of love and respect had anything to do with him
getting to the place where he could say, "I have enough. I don't
need anything"? Do you suppose if you had Jacob's attitude or
Abraham's attitude, that it would change the quality of your
life? I think it would.

In Malachi 3, it says that for the tither with the right attitude, God will open the windows of heaven and pour out blessings that there will not be room enough to contain.

The Lamsa translation says, **. . . I will open the windows of heaven for you and pour out blessings for you until you shall say, It is enough.**

An unending cycle

. . . But now the Lord says, Be it far from Me. For those who honor Me I will honor . . .

I Samuel 2:30
The Amplified Bible

God blessed Abraham so Abraham gave back to God. God blesses you, you give back to Him the tithe out of love and respect. God says, "Oh, somebody has just honored me. He who honors Me, I will honor. So here comes increase!" And then you say, "Look at the increase God brought to me, I'll honor him with the tenth!" And God says, "They've honored me again and whoever honors me, I will honor them." It's an unending cycle. That's what you could call continual prosperity.

God never intended for you and I to live from financial miracle to financial miracle. God wants us to live in continual prosperity until we get to the point where we can say we have enough.

Tithing is the consistent practice of giving back to the God Who has given to you. You're reciprocating out of love not out of command; and consequently, the more you give, the more that comes back to you. Tithers who give with the right attitude attract abundance. Abundance will seek you out.

Don't tithe out of fear. Don't tithe out of religious obligation. If you are, then you're missing the whole point of tithing. Get to a place in your life where you want to tithe because you love God so much and you're so grateful for what He's done in your life. Tithing is an issue of the heart. When you're attitude about tithing is right, the blessings will come and you have placed yourself in a position for a supernatural breakthrough.

3 The determining factor for your breakthrough

In the third visitation of the Lord, He reminded me of the steps which He had revealed to me in the message on supernatural increase and restoration, but this time, He added something. This is what Jesus brought to my attention in that little room in Liberty, Texas. He reminded me of the three things required for a supernatural breakthrough and said, "Teach this to My people," which I've shared in a previous chapter.

Let's look at them once again:

#1. **A prophetic word from God.**

We see again that before there can be a supernatural breakthrough in your life, particularly in the arena of finances, there must first come a prophetic word from God.

You must hear from God. Again, that prophetic word can also be translated into a rhema from God. We have already discovered how to get into position to hear that word from

God. You must spend time with Him. That means you're going to have to turn the television off, put the magazine down, and schedule time to be in His presence. What God may tell you to do may not be what He would tell me to do. You've got to know the mind of God for **your** situation.

Remember, the first thing that God told Elijah to do with the widow woman was to speak the prophetic word: **"For thus saith the Lord God."**

The prophet's word to her was going to change her circumstances dramatically. She was going to go from "not enough" to "more than enough."

#2. **There must be a willingness to obey.**

If God used me to give someone a word of knowledge for their life and they walked off and never did what God instructed them to do, then the breakthrough will not come. The prophetic word is not just going to automatically come to pass. It requires your obedience.

I've had people say to me, "Well, I had somebody prophesy over me 30 years ago and it never came to pass."

"Well, did you ever do what they said you needed to do?"

"No, I just figured if it was God, it would just happen."

That isn't the way it works. It is the will of God that all men be saved, but there are a lot of folks going to hell. Why?

Because they're not doing what He said, **That if thou shalt confess with thy mouth the Lord Jesus, and shall believe in thine heart that God hath raised him from the dead, thou shall be saved** (Romans 10:9).

There must be a willingness to obey. You've got to be willing to obey what God tells you to do. The Bible revealed to us that this woman *went and did* according to the words of Elijah which he had given her from the Lord.

#3. **Sow a seed.**

I have never known of a financial breakthrough where there wasn't first a significant seed sown.

Throughout the Bible, we find that God's people seem to be need-minded and God is seed-minded. Every time I've ever gone to God about a need, if I hang around long enough, He'll talk to me about a seed. That's just the way God operates.

What about my needs?

One time, I was on my way to Tulsa to speak in a conference. I had just received a call from my director from one of our African offices. We were involved in a project there and had spent several hundred thousand dollars building this project and I thought it was completed, then something else happened and we still needed "a ton" of money to finish it.

I didn't have any more money to put into that project. I'd already spent everything I had. I'm talking about hundreds of thousands of dollars. I didn't have what was required to finish it. They needed more. And we had a deadline.

I had just gotten off the phone with my director and I got on an airplane to fly to Tulsa for a Ministers' Conference. On the way up there, sitting there minding my own business, I just said, "Lord, I need . . ." (I quoted the amount of money I needed) and I said, "I need this amount of money to finish that project and I just want to thank You for it."

He said, "When you get to Tulsa, there will be an elderly couple in that meeting tonight who have a ministry of distributing food to the poor in their community. They are believing Me for a new Maxi-Van to put the food in and take it around their town to give to the poor. Give them that new van you just bought."

So we flew a little further. Once again I said, "Lord I just want to thank You for that money for Africa. Praise God. I just thank You for that money."

He said, "When you get to Tulsa, there will be five preachers in that meeting all of whom have just said to Me, 'God, if You don't give me a Word in that meeting tonight, I am leaving the ministry.'" He told me what to tell all five of them. And then He said, "You tell all five of them you are going to send them one of your suits, and you tell them that the spirit of longevity that is on you will come on them."

So far, I have asked God to meet a need in my life and I was giving away a van and five suits. We flew a little further and I said, "Lord, I just want to thank you for that money."

He said, "When you get to Tulsa . . ."

I said, "I don't want to talk to You any more."

I knew what He was doing. He was setting me up for my breakthrough. Now I want you to notice in each of these situations He talked to me about sowing seed, significant seed. Why? Because my harvest was significant. I didn't need a couple hundred dollars. The harvest I needed was a large amount of money. So He told me to sow those seeds. That was the prophetic Word or the rhema from God.

When I got to Tulsa, they turned the service over to me and I began preaching. The Spirit of God said, "Stop and do what I told you to do." So I just stopped in the middle of the service and I said, "There is a couple in here and you have a ministry of distributing food to the poor and you've asked God for a new Maxi-Van, one of those large vans, to distribute this food. Would you please stand up?"

This elderly couple stood up with tears running down their cheeks. I said, "Would you please come up here?" They came to the front and I said, "I just want you to know that I bought your van a couple of weeks ago. I thought I was buying it for my ministry but the Lord told me that I bought it for yours and if you'll follow me to Fort Worth after this meeting, I'll give it to you debt free."

Oh, they just broke out in tears of joy and rejoicing as well as everybody else.

And then I said, "There are five preachers in here from different places around the country, and all five of you left your house this morning saying that if you didn't get a word from God in this meeting, you were going to leave the ministry. Would all five of you preachers stand up?"

All five of them stood up. Miraculously, there wasn't a tall one in the bunch. All five of them were my size. Every one of them. I called all five of them up and told them what God told me to tell them about the suits. As soon as I got home, I laid hands on five suits and then sent each of them one.

A significant seed had to be sown to establish a point of contact to release my faith. In the story of the widow woman, she had already told the prophet that all she had was a little cake. He told her that the little cake would do. **"Bring me a cake first."**

I would call that little cake a **significant seed.** In her case, it was all she had. God may not require you to sow all you have. However, the only time a little seed will produce a large harvest is when it is all you have. Otherwise, it is a violation of spiritual law: "sow sparingly and you reap sparingly. Sow bountifully and you reap bountifully" (2 Corinthians 9:26).

I did what God told me to do in Tulsa that night and the next day I returned home and I received a phone call. My secretary said, "Brother Jerry, this man says that you're not really close friends, but he had met you in some meetings where you preached and he wants to know if he can talk to you." I got on the phone and he reminded me of where I had met him and I did remember him.

He said, "My wife and I have really been blessed by your ministry. We're young at walking in the Spirit and being led by the Spirit and we just wanted to call and ask your advice."

I said, "O.K."

He said, "We were praying last night at five o'clock." (five o'clock was when I was flying to Tulsa and saying, "Lord, I need this . . . I need this harvest.")

He said, "We were praying last night at five o'clock and we have a significant amount to sow and your name keeps coming up. We just want to know if this figure means anything to you." It was exactly what I needed! They sent it overnight express and my breakthrough came!

That supernatural breakthrough came as a result of a significant seed sown.

Before my visitation ended in that room in Liberty, Texas, Jesus said, "Tell them if they will apply the spiritual laws I have just shared with you, that the God of the Breakthrough will visit their house!"

I said, "Lord, will You show me from the Scripture what happens when God visits somebody's house?" He led me to Genesis 5:24.

This is Joseph speaking just before he was about to die:

And Joseph said unto his brethren, I die: and God

will surely visit you, and bring you out of this land unto the land which he sware to Abraham, to Isaac, and to Jacob.

Genesis 50:24

God will surely visit you and **bring you out**. When God visits your house, get ready! You are coming out of something! Hallelujah.

Something that has held you back. Something that has kept you down. Something that has limited and restricted you. When God visits your house, things start changing! Why? Because He is the God of the breakthrough!

He said, "Tell the people to do what I'm telling you to tell them." I encourage you to receive the prophetic word that God will visit your house. Be willing to obey, and then sow a significant seed as a point of contact to release your faith.

Finally, He said, "Tell them this. Once they release that seed, then the depth of their praise will determine the magnitude of their breakthrough."

In other words, if all you do is put this book down and say, "Well, wasn't that a nice little book that little preacher wrote." Then there's no depth in that. But if you go to bed tonight, before you close your eyes, and declare, "The God of the Breakthrough is going to visit my house. The God of the Breakthrough is going to visit my house." And then when you wake up in the morning, the first thing that comes out of your mouth is, "Glory to God. The God of the Breakthrough is about to visit my house," then your breakthrough is on the horizon!

Go through the day shouting, "The God of the Breakthrough is visiting my house." The depth of your praise will determine the magnitude of your breakthrough! Be consistent with your confession, your faith and your expectancy.

Do you receive this prophetic word from the Lord? If you do, then get ready, you're coming out.

Are you willing to obey the prophetic word that you just received?

Are you ready to sow a significant seed? Significant would imply that it has special meaning to you. David said, "I will not give God an offering . . . which cost me nothing" (2 Samuel 24:24).

Don't give God a token, give Him a significant seed and then watch how the God of the Breakthrough will come through for **You**!

The God of the breakthrough is visiting my house!

"Father, in the Name of Jesus, I,_____ ,
declare by faith that on this date, _____ ,
I have received a prophetic word from You, and I am going
to be obedient. I release my faith right now as I sow a significant seed for my breakthrough. This seed is my point of contact, and I believe that every seed produces after its own
kind. I am believing for a breakthrough in
my_____ . Thank You, Father,
for being the God of the breakthrough and for visiting my
house, in Jesus' Name. Amen."

If this message has touched your life and you would like to
sow your seed into Jerry Savelle Ministries, please tear out
this page and send it to:

Jerry Savelle Ministries International
P.O. Box 748
Crowley, TX 76036
817/297-3155
Or check our website for the office nearest you at
www.jsmi.org

Send us your testimonies of breakthrough!

About the author

Dr. Jerry Savelle is a noted author, evangelist, pastor, and teacher who travels extensively throughout the United States, and around the globe. He is president of Jerry Savelle Ministries International, a ministry of many outreaches devoted to bringing the lost to Christ and meeting the needs of Believers all over the world.

Well known for his balanced Biblical teaching Dr. Savelle has conducted seminars, crusades and conventions for over thirty years as well as ministering in thousands of churches and fellowships. He is in great demand today because of his inspiring message of victory and faith and his vivid, and often humorous, illustrations from the Bible. He teaches the Word of God in a simple, down-to-earth style that proves God can take the average person and make them extraordinary.

In addition to his International Headquarters in Crowley, Texas, Dr. Savelle has also established offices in the United Kingdom, South Africa, Tanzania, Singapore, Australia, and Botswana in order to reach the nations with the life-changing message of Jesus. Dr. Savelle also established a Correspondence School, which he refers to as "the School without walls" for those desiring a deeper foundation in the Word. He also pastors a church with his wife, Carolyn, in Crowley, Texas, called Heritage of Faith Christian Center.

The missions outreaches of his ministry extend to over fifty countries around the world.

Dr. Savelle has written over forty books and has an extensive video and cassette teaching tape ministry and a nationwide television broadcast, **Adventures in Faith**. Thousands of books, tapes, and videos are distributed around the world every year through Jerry Savelle Ministries International.

To order related material,
call, write or visit our website
for further information.

Jerry Savelle Ministries International
P.O. Box 748
Crowley, TX 76036
817/297-3155
www.jsmi.org

Other books by Jerry Savelle

For those who don't know Jesus, would you like to know Him?

If you were to die today, where would you spend eternity? If you have accepted Jesus Christ as your personal Lord and Savior, you can be assured that when you die, you will go directly into the presence of God in Heaven. If you have not accepted Jesus as your personal Lord and Savior, is there any reason why you can't make Jesus the Lord of your life right now? Please pray this prayer out loud, and as you do, pray with a sincere and trusting heart, and you will be born again.

Dear God in Heaven,

I come to You in the Name of Jesus to receive salvation and eternal life. I believe that Jesus is Your Son. I believe that He died on the cross for my sins, and that You raised Him from the dead. I receive Jesus now into my heart and make Him the Lord of my life. Jesus, come into my heart. I welcome You as my Lord and Savior. Father, I believe Your Word that says I am now saved. I confess with my mouth that I am saved and born again. I am now a child of God.